JEWELS
OF THE KINGDOM

Discover Hidden Treasure in God's Word
and the Treasure You Are to Him

I0080512

Kathleen VonSeggern

ELECTRIC
MOON
PUBLISHING

I'm delighted to recommend this book, authored by a respected figure in our faith community. It's a potential study guide for both new believers and those who have matured in their faith, making it a valuable addition to any church library.

Whether you've been walking with God for a considerable time or have just embarked on your new life in Christ, this book is a must-read. It caters to all, offering insights and wisdom that can enrich your understanding, regardless of your familiarity with a life dedicated to following our Lord and Savior, Jesus Christ.

Regardless of where you are in your faith journey, this book is a powerful testament to the transformative power of choosing to follow Jesus. The author, in a deeply personal and relatable manner, shares her own journey, a narrative that will inspire and connect with believers at all stages and the kingdom principles she has discovered along the way.

Within its pages you'll find a wealth of biblical examples and practical principles designed not just for intellectual understanding but also for continued growth and development in your faith journey. This book is not just educational; it's transformational, empowering you with practical tools for those who seek a deeper relationship with Jesus.

—*Apostle Dr. Marshall McGee*
Presiding Apostle, Kingdom Mandate Fellowship (Global)

I dedicate this book to the person of the
Holy Spirit, without whom none of
this would have been possible.

CONTENTS

ACKNOWLEDGMENTS

I would like to extend my deepest gratitude to the following people:

To my husband, Clayton—you have steadfastly continued to believe in me, pray for me, and support me with love and encouragement throughout this incredible journey.

To the Treasures of the Heart Ministry prayer team—your collective dedication and countless hours of prayer have been a powerful source of strength and inspiration. Your role in the success of the ministry and this book is immeasurable. Your prayers have truly made a profound difference, and I am deeply grateful for your impactful and effective support.

Thank you to Sue Sundstrom for igniting the flame within my heart with your encouragement, understanding, and grace—and to my fellow authors, Lauri Gruen, Elisha Janine, Hilary Taylorson, and Adele Best, for your never-ending prayers, kind words, constructive feedback, and unwavering support. Each of you has played a unique and significant role in this journey, and I am deeply grateful for your contributions.

Thank you, Dori Minchow-Stubbendeck, for making the picture in my head a beautiful reality on the cover of this book. Your artistic talent and dedication have enhanced the book's visual appeal and played a significant role in its success. I deeply admire your artistic skills and the beauty you have brought to this book.

To all my family and friends—your encouragement, kind words, constructive feedback, prayers, and unwavering support have been a constant source of strength. I am deeply grateful for every one of you.

I appreciate your consistent guidance and perseverance, Laree Lindburg and Electric Moon Publishing. Thank you for your prayers and encouragement during this process and for your significant role in the success of this book.

INTRODUCTION

Jewels of the Kingdom is written based on years of countless hours spent in prayer and communion with God. I have written it from a heart captivated by God's love and cultivated by His grace. In this book you will be led on an adventure as you search the treasure chest of God's Word to discover the treasure He has placed within you, a treasure that was always meant to be shared, as the Holy Spirit unlocks and polishes the jewels hidden within you, His bride.

Each chapter invites you on a journey to deeper intimacy with Christ as I guide you on a treasure hunt through the Word of God to explore the map of God's unique plan for your life.

Enjoy the journey as the Holy Spirit leads you into the true revelation of your God-given identity.

1
LOVE

There's Plenty to Go Around

LOVE: INTRODUCTION

God is love. So love is the heart of heaven, and exploring its treasure could be the most rewarding adventure you will ever take.

Love transcends language barriers, expressing itself in word and deed as we look for the gold in others. Yet extending such love can be a challenge, especially if we fail to grasp the intentional nature of God's love for us. Why? Because we can give only what we truly possess.

Until the age of seven, I had heard about God but never personally experienced who He is. Dad worked in construction, so we moved wherever work could be found. Mom would read us Bible stories and find a church for us to attend in our new location. Dad did not go to church with us, but one Sunday he decided to join us. After the service he told the pastor that he wanted to give his life to Christ. Our life as we knew it changed that day. I as a young girl noticed the change that took place in my dad's life, which became a ripple effect on our family. One year later I asked Jesus to come live in my own heart. Falling in love with Jesus was easy after witnessing the *radical* change that had taken place in our home. But realizing God's love for me took years. Because being *told* you are loved by God and *knowing* you are loved are two entirely different things. When I know I am loved, I walk in complete confidence of where I stand with the one who loves me.

Becoming captivated by God's love for me did not happen overnight. It was a process of believing the truth of God's Word and what it said about His love for me. As a teenager I became intrigued with the Word of God and couldn't seem to get enough of it. As years passed and the trials of life seemed to engulf me, God's Word and His love for me continued to prove true. My character grew in the midst of the trials as I continued setting time aside each day to spend time with God and embrace His Word. Thus, I have become captivated by His love for me.

Remember the wonders he has performed, his
miracles and rulings he has given.
(Psalm 105:5 NLT)

Nothing will ever stop God from loving you. He gave his only Son for you because giving up on you was never an option. Discover the precious gem of God's love for you as we mine the hidden treasures in His Word together.

FROM HEAD TO TOE

Have you ever heard someone say, "I hurt from head to toe"? Unfortunately, it is a common expression that we can all relate to.

However, we are told in Mark 15:15–20 of a man *who chose* to experience intense pain throughout His entire body, beyond what we can imagine. Soldiers beat Him with a whip made of leather straps embedded with metal. A crown of thorns was placed on His head, driven deeply into His brow, while being repeatedly hit on His head with a reed staff, spit on, and ridiculed. Finally His hands and feet were nailed to a cross, where He hung for hours, feeling as if God had abandoned Him. Yet amidst His pain, with a heart full of compassion and love at His last breath, He asked God to forgive those who had abused and mistreated Him.

When we are hurting amid the storms of life, it's easy to forget who carried the most pain and the heaviest cross. His name is Jesus, and He did it for you. No one will ever love you so much that he or she would pay such an enormous price for you to be forgiven of your sin.

He is despised and rejected by men, a Man
of sorrows and acquainted with grief. And we
hid, as it were, our faces from Him; He was
despised, and we did not esteem Him. Surely He
has borne our griefs and carried our sorrows;
Yet we esteemed Him stricken, smitten by God,
and afflicted. But He was wounded for our

transgressions, He was bruised for our iniquities;
the chastisement for our peace was upon Him,
and by His stripes we are healed.

(Isaiah 53:3–5 NKJV)

STUDY GUIDE
Mark 15:15–39; John 3:16

PERSONAL REFLECTION

1. What does the cross Jesus carried mean to you personally?
2. Which part of the price Jesus paid relates to what you are going through today?

LISTEN FOR THE HEARTBEAT

In the gospel of John the apostle and author referred to himself as "the disciple Jesus loved" five times. He is the only disciple we are told of who laid his head on Jesus' chest (John 13:23). In that moment I believe he heard the heartbeat of the Father beating in the rhythm of love for him.

"I will be a Father to you, and you shall be My sons and daughters, says the Lord Almighty."
(2 Corinthians 6:18 NKJV)

John's identity was established as the disciple Jesus loved. Therefore John no longer functioned as an orphan but as a child of God. Because he knew the Father's love for him, he lived by faith that everything that belonged to Jesus as a Son also belonged to him.

On the other hand, the apostle Peter took a different approach. He continually tried to prove his love for Jesus through his actions. The contrast in these two disciples' approaches is significant, as it shows that instead of focusing on Jesus, Peter was preoccupied with his own performance, constantly striving to demonstrate to Jesus how much he loved Him.

Jesus, asked Peter three times, "Peter, do you love me?" Each time Peter affirmed his love. Jesus then responded, "Then feed my sheep and follow me." This interaction was a powerful reminder to Peter that *if he would shift his focus from self-performance to Jesus Himself,* then Jesus' love for Peter would radiate through him, transforming his actions and interactions with others. This story is a beacon of hope, illustrating the life-changing power of God's love in our lives.

When we are able to shift our focus, freeing ourselves from the constraints of performance-based love and instead embracing God's love for us by laying our heads upon His chest and hearing His heartbeat in the rhythm of love, we will begin thinking and acting like children of a king. This shift in perspective empowers us to search for and walk out the destiny that was written in the scrolls of heaven about us before we were even formed in our mothers' wombs.

God showed how much he loved us by sending his one and only Son into the world so that we might have eternal life through him. This is real love—not that we loved God but that he loved us and sent his Son as a sacrifice to take away our sins.

(1 John 4:9–10 NLT)

STUDY GUIDE

John 13:23; John 21:15–17; Psalm 139:16; Luke 9:33

PERSONAL REFLECTION

1. Has your focus been on proving your love for God through performance?
2. How might your perspective change if you leaned your head upon Jesus' chest as John did and listen to His heartbeat?

THE UNIVERSAL LANGUAGE

Some of us have spent most of our lives looking for love in all the wrong places, which has led only to heartache and disappointment. Perhaps all we have ever known is abuse and rejection by those who were supposed to love and care about us.

It is hard to imagine the kind of love that would cause someone to lay his or her life down for us. And it is hard to love those who do not love us back. But God loved the world so much that He gave His only Son to die on a cross so that you could be forgiven and live eternally in heaven with Him.

"I am persuaded that neither death nor life, nor angels nor principalities nor powers, nor things present nor things to come, nor height nor depth, nor any other created thing, shall be able to separate us from the love of God which is in Christ Jesus our Lord."
(Romans 8:38–39 NKJV)

What is love? In 1 Corinthians 13:4–7 we are told, "Love is patient and kind. Love is not jealous or boastful or proud or rude. It does not demand its own way. It is not irritable, and it keeps no record of being wronged. It does not rejoice about injustice but rejoices whenever the truth wins out. Love never gives up, never loses faith, is always hopeful, and endures through every circumstance" (NLT). No matter what language we speak, love is the only universal language. God's love will always be there for us.

What kind of world would it be if we could all *open our hearts to accept* the love of a heavenly Father who loves us unconditionally? What kind of world would it be if we could love and see others through our heavenly Father's eyes?

"This is how God loved the world: He gave his one and only Son, so that everyone who believes in him will not perish but have eternal life. God sent his Son into the world not to judge the world, but to save the world through him."

(John 3:16–17 NLT)

STUDY GUIDE
Isaiah 53; 1 Corinthians 13:4–7

PERSONAL REFLECTION
1. Have you been looking for love in all the wrong places?
2. Have you ever experienced or loved someone with the kind of love described in these passages?

FOR THE LOVE OF GOD

What we love—we treasure. God desires for us to live from a valued position with Him. He wants us to be free of self-rejection and pride because we cannot fully love ourselves or others until we accept His love for us.

The more time we spend with someone, the better we get to know him or her. God desires that we spend time with Him, thus becoming like Him and living from a place of love.

"And you shall love the LORD your God with all your heart, with all your soul, with all your mind, and with all your strength.' This is the first commandment. And the second, like it, is this: 'You shall love your neighbor as yourself.' There is no other commandment greater than these."
(Mark 12:30–31 NKJV)

How can we love others as we love ourselves when most of us struggle with self-acceptance? Charity begins at home, and you can't give what you don't have. Therefore, we need to *stop devaluing what God has created*. When others attack someone or something very precious to us, it is as if they are attacking a part of us. When we speak words against ourselves or others, God feels the pain. It breaks His heart because we are made by the hand of God, created in His image. Our value begins there. Who are we to argue with God about how He made us or anyone else?

"By their fruits you will know them. Not everyone who says to Me, 'Lord, Lord,' shall enter the kingdom of heaven, but he who does the will of My Father in heaven. Many will say to Me in that day, 'Lord, Lord, have we not prophesied in Your name, cast out demons in Your name, and done many wonders in Your name?' And then I will declare to them, 'I never knew you; depart from Me, you who practice lawlessness!'"

(Matthew 7:20–23 NKJV)

I wonder if He will also say, "Yes, you did all these things, but did you do them in love? Because if it wasn't in love, it was just a big waste of time!"

STUDY GUIDE

Mark 15:15–20; John 3:16; 1 John 4:15–20; Romans 9:20

PERSONAL REFLECTION

1. Do you see yourself as God sees you?
2. Are you aware of how precious you are to God and how much He loves you? If not, why not?

MY FATHER'S EYES

The more time we spend with someone, the better we get to know the person. We may even begin to replicate some of that person's character. What if the world started to look at us and not only saw a reflection of Jesus but also longed for the Jesus in us? Because the more time we spend with Him, the more we become like Him.

In Mark 8:22–25 we read about a blind man who was brought to Jesus for healing. Jesus took the blind man by the hand and led him out of town. Then after spitting on the man's eyes and touching them, Jesus asked the man if he could see. The man looked up and told Jesus that he saw men but could not see them clearly—they looked like trees walking. Jesus touched the man's eyes again, and the man's eyesight was completely restored. Jesus then sent the man home, telling him not to return to the village on his way.

What if another touch from Jesus would cause us to see others for who God created them to be—not judging them by the shapes of their bodies, the color of their skin, the language they speak, or the clothes they wear? Instead, we would see them through our heavenly Father's eyes, knowing that we are all a work in progress created by the hand of God.

Spending time with Jesus can develop His character in us so that we will no longer see men as trees walking but see them through the eyes of the Creator. His touch may not always come in the way you expect, but it will always come in love.

*"The Lord doesn't see things the way you see them.
People judge by outward appearance,
but the Lord looks at the heart."*

(1 Samuel 16:7 NLT)

STUDY GUIDE
Mark 8:22–25; 1 Samuel 16:4–13; Isaiah 64:8

PERSONAL REFLECTION
1. Are you looking through your heavenly Father's eyes?
2. Ask God to give you a heart of compassion and love to see clearly. Journal your thoughts.

REJECTED BY MAN

In Matthew 8:1–3 we read about a man who followed Jesus and His disciples from a distance and listened to every word Jesus spoke. He watched as the sick, blind, and lame were healed. This man longed for a touch from Jesus because leprosy had invaded his body. For years he could see only from a distance those he loved. He longed for human contact, but people ran from leprosy. The man was rejected, alone, and lonely, but hope began rising within him for the first time in years. If only he could get close enough for Jesus to see him—then perhaps Jesus would have compassion on him and speak healing words.

But if he got close, would Jesus see the bitter person he had become? Would Jesus even want to heal him? He had heard stories about Jesus, how He loved those who didn't deserve to be loved. Were they true? If only the man could get the nerve to come out of hiding, he would ask Jesus to heal him.

When He had come down from the mountain, great multitudes followed Him. And behold, a leper came and worshiped Him, saying, "Lord, if You are willing, You can make me clean." Then Jesus put out His hand and touched him, saying, "I am willing; be cleansed." Immediately his leprosy was cleansed.

(Matthew 8:1–3 NKJV)

Leprosy was so contagious in those days that people with the disease had to leave their communities and live outside of town. Contact with people free of the disease was not permitted. But Jesus' love and compassion for this man was so profound that He willingly reached out to him. I can only imagine the intensity of love this man felt when the Son of God touched him as healing flowed from His hand. They had never met, yet Jesus with a heart full of compassion, and love touched the man and made him well.

He heals the brokenhearted and bandages their wounds.

(Psalm 147:3 NLT)

STUDY GUIDE
Luke 5:12–16; Romans 8:38–39

PERSONAL REFLECTION

1. Do you feel unworthy of God's love for you?
2. Do you live in fear of rejection? Journal your thoughts.

A NEW WAY TO LOVE

*God is love, and he who abides in
love abides in God, and God in him.*
(1 John 4:16 NKJV)

Humans have not yet fully realized God's love. We frequently use the word *love* in place of *like*. For example, I *love* chocolate, the color red, or baseball. In today's society the love of self-satisfaction is more important than the act of kindness. Our love for God is often disguised as service to Him rather than longing for a deeper relationship with Him.

In John 18:10–11 we read about Peter's attempt to prove his love for Jesus by slicing off the high priest's servant's ear. However, Jesus' reaction to Peter's courage was not as Peter had expected as He told Peter to put his sword away. Then Jesus lovingly reached out and healed the ear of the man, who had come to arrest Him.

Despite his imperfections, Peter was chosen by Jesus to lead future generations to a saving knowledge of Jesus Christ and His love. Jesus saw beyond Peter's outward flaws and recognized the love in his heart. This recognition led Peter to love Jesus in his own way—until Jesus revealed a new, deeper way to love. When Peter truly understood and felt Jesus' love for him, he was then able to love others through the Spirit of Christ within him.

Love is not just a feeling but also a deep understanding of God and His love for us. It is about reflecting His love in our daily lives by spending time with Him. When we wholeheartedly love God, we are compelled to worship Him. Therefore, we must align our hearts in faith, fully believing in His identity, because true worship is a matter of the heart.

"The time is coming—indeed it's here now—when true worshipers will worship the Father in spirit and in truth. The Father is looking for those who will worship him that way. For God is Spirit, so those who worship him must worship in spirit and in truth."

(John 4:23–24 NLT)

STUDY GUIDE

John 18:10; Mark 3:13–16; John 21:15–19; Mark 12:30–31

PERSONAL REFLECTION

1. How often have you reacted as Peter did, by striking out at those who disagree with you?
2. In what way could your heart change in this area?

BROKEN VESSEL

We read in Luke 7:36–50 that Jesus was having dinner at the home of Simon, a Pharisee, when a woman known as a prostitute brought an alabaster jar of expensive fragrant oil and stood behind Jesus weeping. She began washing His feet with her tears and wiped them with her hair. Then she kissed His feet and anointed them with the fragrant oil.

Despite the fact that the woman was fully aware of her past and totally repentant of it, those sitting around the table made sure that Jesus knew of her reputation and unworthiness to be near Him. The alabaster jar represented everything of value to her and the broken vessel that she was. But because of her deep love for Jesus, she was willing to give up everything she had. This woman's focus was not on herself but on her love for Jesus and His forgiveness of her sin.

Although Luke does not tell us the woman's name, we are told in John 11:2 that her name was Mary; she was the sister of Lazarus and Martha. We are also told in Luke 10:38–42 about Mary as she sat at the feet of Jesus with her focus only on Him—as her sister, Martha, rushed about preparing a meal.

Like Mary, we all have an alabaster jar filled with things we have treasured throughout our lives. Perhaps our alabaster jar represents the place we have become accustomed to, where we have accepted the label others have put on us or we have placed on ourselves.

When we can fully accept and receive God's compassionate love for us, it is then that we will come with a heart of humble repentance, proclaiming our love for Him. As we focus on His beauty and grace, we will no longer only seek His hand for what He can do for us, but we will also long to seek His face—discovering more of who He is and the treasure of His love for us.

"Do not lay up for yourselves treasures on earth, where moth and rust destroy and where thieves break in and steal; but lay up for yourselves treasures in heaven, where neither moth nor rust destroys and where thieves do not break in and steal. For where your treasure is, there your heart will be also."

(Matthew 6:19–21 NKJV)

STUDY GUIDE

Luke 7:36–50; John 11:2; Luke 10:38–42; Romans 5:6–11

PERSONAL REFLECTION

1. What is in your alabaster jar?
2. Are you focused on what others think of you? Journal your thoughts.

SWEATING BLOOD

While Jesus was in the garden before going to the cross, overwhelmed by what lay ahead in the coming hours, we read in Luke 22:44–46 that His sweat fell to the ground like drops of blood. *We often overlook the price that He paid in prayer for our fear and anxiety.*

Then they came to a place which was named Gethsemane;
and He said to His disciples, "Sit here while I pray."
And He took Peter, James, and John with Him, and He
began to be troubled and deeply distressed. Then
He said to them, "My soul is exceedingly sorrowful,
even to death. Stay here and watch."
(Mark 14:32–34 NKJV)

Many times I have felt overwhelmed by anxiety and fear. But then I refocus my thoughts and position my heart on Jesus, knowing that my name is engraved in the palm of His hand. I can see His nail-scared hands, and I imagine myself standing where they placed the nails.

It is easy to get overwhelmed with fear and anxiety in a world filled with anger, violence, and the loss of individual identity and innocence. But when we look at the nail print in His hand and envision His sweating drops of blood while praying in the garden before going to the cross, we can rest assured that He has already paid for whatever we may encounter.

As humans, we find it hard to imagine someone loving us so much that the person would willingly sweat drops of blood for us, much less be nailed to a cross. Even though Jesus knew the intensity He felt in the garden was only a prelude to what was to come because of His unconditional love for us, He was willing to pay the price in full for our freedom.

From God's first breath into Adam, our spirit was created in the heart of God before our soul came to be. Therefore He has loved us since the beginning of time with an everlasting love. And there isn't anything we can do to change that!

"I have inscribed you on the palms of My hands;
Your walls are continually before Me."
(Isaiah 49:16 NKJV)

STUDY GUIDE
Luke 22:44–46; Genesis 2:7; 1 John 4:10;
Jeremiah 31:3; Philippians 4:6–7

PERSONAL REFLECTION
1. Do you worry a lot? Picture Jesus in the garden sweating drops of blood for everything you fear.
2. Now picture your name written in the palm of Jesus' hand where the nail print is. Journal your thoughts.

THERE'S ALWAYS ROOM FOR MORE

Many envision God as a stern, authoritative being who sits in a judgment seat in heaven. Yet we are reminded throughout Scripture that God is love. I can imagine Jesus walking down the road with His disciples, joking and laughing, sometimes stopping to skip rocks on the water. Jesus often went out of His way to reach those in need. He had compassion for everyone He encountered.

But Jesus wasn't a pushover—He stood up for what was right and spoke out against injustice. A lot of people try to do this, but Jesus did more. He represented the Father in all He did, and He said only what He heard His Father say. He always spoke the truth in love and was not afraid to reveal sin.

At that time the disciples came to Jesus, saying, "Who then is greatest in the kingdom of heaven?" Then Jesus called a little child to Him, set him in the midst of them, and said, "Assuredly, I say to you, unless you are converted and become as little children, you will by no means enter the kingdom of heaven. Therefore whoever humbles himself as this little child is the greatest in the kingdom of heaven. Whoever receives one little child like this in My name receives Me. But whoever causes one of these little ones who believe in Me to sin, it would be better for him if a millstone were hung around his neck, and he were drowned in the depth of the sea."
(Matthew 18:1–6 NKJV)

One day while I was praying for children, I envisioned Jesus sitting in heaven's courts, and children were coming by the multitudes to sit on His lap. As they came, Jesus' lap kept expanding until it was large enough to hold them all. His arms reached to wrap around each one as they came. I then began praying for teens and adults. As I envisioned them coming closer to Jesus, they became children again as they sat on His lap. There was room for everyone and plenty of His love to go around. Then I saw the angels as they stood arm in arm around God's throne, the fire of God surrounded them. And Jesus said, "Let the children come to me. Don't stop them! For the kingdom of heaven belongs to those who are like these children."

During His three short years of ministry on earth, Jesus' love for the Father and others made such a mark on society that we are still talking about it today. No one has ever loved as He loved. Jesus replicated the Father in everything He said and did.

As you come to Him with childlike faith, there will always be room for you in the arms of Jesus. You don't have to wait until you pass from this life to get there. He is available now, and He is waiting for you. Will you come?

"They shall be Mine," says the Lord of hosts,
"On the day that I make them My jewels.
And I will spare them
as a man spares his own son who serves him."
(Malachi 3:17 NKJV)

STUDY GUIDE

Matthew 10:14; Matthew 7:6; Ephesians 4:11–16;
Matthew 19:13–14; John 5:19

PERSONAL REFLECTION

1. Try to imagine the kind of Father you always dreamed of having.
2. Now imagine yourself as a child, sitting on the lap of Jesus. As He wraps His arms around you, can you feel His love for you? Journal your thoughts.

LIFE APPLICATION

Heavenly Father,

Thank you for loving me just as I am. Help me to accept the treasure of your love for me and the gem I am to you so that I can love others as you love me. Father, I pray that you will become the passion of my heart so that I will see myself and others through your eyes and that all will know who my heavenly Father is because of your love shining through me for them.

In your name I pray.

Amen

2
PRAYER

Stop Defying Gravity

PRAYER: INTRODUCTION

Touching heaven through the treasure of prayer is a privilege we are all granted. Being alone with the Father was so important to Jesus that He often withdrew to secluded places where He could pray. It is there where Jesus drew strength, encouragement, and character from the Father's spirit to His.

Moving from place to place throughout my childhood, I was always the new kid in a different school and never belonged anywhere. The feeling of rejection became a part of who I was. While other children ate lunch and played on the playground together, the new girl was often alone. We never stayed in one place long enough for us to make friends. And after a while I felt like *Why try?*

When I asked Jesus to live in my heart at age eight, a change occurred, and Jesus became my best friend, whom I could take with me when we moved to a new place, who would never talk about me behind my back, make fun of me, or reject me—a friend who loved me just as I was. I could speak to Him about anything. Thus began my prayer life and a relationship with God the Father, His Son Jesus, and the Holy Spirit. As I spent time with Him in prayer, our relationship grew, and my love for Him and desire to communicate with Him became intense. Still today I feel honored to be invited to sit with the King of kings and the Lord of lords in a quiet place.

As you delve into this chapter, may you discover a fresh perspective on prayer, a divine connection that transcends earthly boundaries. May you, as a member of His bride, embark on a new journey with the three persons of Christ. I pray that you will fall deeply in love with your groom, yearning to spend more time with Him in a quiet place. And always remember—before you step into the battlefield of life, find your rest in Him.

TEACH US TO PRAY

Jesus led by example. Thus, He did not teach His disciples to preach. He taught them to *pray*—because He knew that if they could pray, they would be able to do whatever He called them to do.

"When you pray, do not use vain repetitions as the heathen do For they think that they will be heard for their many words. Therefore do not be like them. For your Father knows the things you have need of before you ask Him."

(Matthew 6:7–8 NKJV)

"Father in Heaven, holy is your name." We are to praise and glorify Him. Remember: God is already aware of the problem, so share with Him what is on your heart and then express your gratitude for the forthcoming answer.

"Your kingdom come, your will be done on earth as it is in heaven." Pray the word of God back to the God who wrote it. Give Him the situation, humble yourself, and get out of the way.

"Give us this day our daily bread." Ask Him to supply your needs and accept and receive what He has for you, knowing that you are His child and that He loves you.

"Forgive us our trespasses, as we forgive those who trespass against us." Walk in forgiveness for others, letting go of grudges and resentment and accept God's forgiveness for you.

"Lead us not into temptation but deliver us from evil." Give up doubt, fear, and unbelief. Trust God to guide you.

"For yours is the kingdom, the power, and the glory forever." We should always remember who He is. And praise Him that He hears and listens to your prayers!

The earnest prayer of a righteous person has great power and produces wonderful results.

(James 5:16 NLT)

STUDY GUIDE

Psalm 150:6; Romans 8:28; Philippians 4:19;
Matthew 6:14–15; 1 Corinthians 10:13; Psalm 103:1–5

PERSONAL REFLECTION

1. Are you praying the way Jesus taught us to pray?
2. How can you change your prayer life to model the prayer of Jesus?

HEARING HIS VOICE

One of the most frequent questions I have been asked through the years is "How does one discern and understand the voice of God?" This question, often with a mix of curiosity and longing, has led me to share my personal experiences and insights.

From a young age, I began to distinguish the voices of my parents and siblings. Over time, these voices became familiar to me. In a similar way, our relationship with God is built on personal experiences that help us recognize His voice.

In 1 Samuel 3:1–10 we read that God called Samuel three times one night before Samuel or Eli, the priest, realized it was God. Then Eli instructed Samuel to answer God's call to him by saying, "Speak, Lord. Your servant is listening." This story reminds us of the patience and persistence of God's call, reassuring us that He will not give up on us.

"My sheep hear My voice,
and I know them, and they follow Me."
(John 10:27 NKJV)

My communion with God has taught me that His voice becomes more recognizable with time. He speaks in the stillness, in a gentle whisper that only those who truly listen can hear. His voice may also be found in a song, an act of kindness, or a stranger's comforting words. And most importantly, He speaks through His love letter the Holy Bible, which is a treasure trove of His wisdom and guidance.

Elijah stood on the mountain, and the Lord passed by, thus causing a mighty windstorm to hit the mountain, plus an earthquake and fire, but the Lord was not in any of these things, although when Elijah stood still he could hear the whisper of the Lord.

However God speaks, it is always from a heart of love for us and never goes against His Word. Sometimes, I tell people to pay attention to the voice to explain how to know if it is God speaking to them, If the voice in your head says, *"I'm* not good enough," that is what you think about yourself. God would never tell you that you are not good enough. If the voice in your head says, *"you are not* good enough," it is being spoken to you from somewhere other than heaven. Your heavenly Father would never talk to you, His beautiful creation, in a negative way that would put you down and discourage you. If the voice tells you, *"You are* fearfully and wonderfully made," God is telling you His thoughts toward you, which are always loving and good.

God loves you so much and cares about even the smallest detail of your life, and He would never tell you anything that contradicts His Word.

I encourage you to spend time alone in a quiet place with Him. As that place becomes more familiar to you, His presence and voice will also become familiar to you. We must remember that spending time alone with God is not about us doing all the talking. To hear His voice, we must be willing to listen. Just be still and know that He is God.

You formed my inward parts; You covered me in my mother's womb. I will praise You, for I am fearfully and wonderfully made; Marvelous are Your works, and that my soul knows very well.

(Psalm 139:13–14 NKJV)

STUDY GUIDE
1 Samuel 3:1–10; Philippians 4:8; Matthew 10:29–31;
1 Kings 19:11–12; Psalm 46:10; John 10:1–16

PERSONAL REFLECTION
1. Do you recognize God's voice?
2. What has God been speaking to you about?

"INSTANT GOD"

We live in an instant world with instant information, meals, and coffee. We often expect instant results in whatever we do. Modern technology has allowed us to connect with others far away and gain information quickly. Some people even develop instant friendships on social media. Many have developed the mindset of having an instant prayer life and Bible reading in this fast-paced life.

God longs to be the center of our lives and cherishes our time with Him. He desires for us to prioritize time with Him daily. Whether we dedicate ten minutes or three hours in prayer or study, what truly matters is the posture of our hearts and the intention behind our actions. To help you in this journey, consider setting a specific time each day, such as early morning or before bed, to spend with God. The key is to find a routine that works for you and stick to it.

"You shall love the Lord your God with all your heart, with all your soul, and with all your mind."
(Matthew 22:37 NKJV)

In this fast-paced world, it's easy to get distracted and lose focus on what is most important. Our focus should not be on man or things but on God, and if we put Him first in our lives, the other things will fall into place. It's not about the quantity of time we spend with the Lord but rather the quality. Have you ever had lunch with someone who wasn't really "present"?

In all appearances, the person is there physically, but his or her mind and heart are somewhere else. Perhaps the person was texting or answering phone calls during your time together. How did that make you feel? Similarly, when we meet with God, He desires our full attention.

Spending quality time with God does not guarantee that we will not have problems. The storms around us may persist, but when we invest in time with Him, it has the power to calm the storm within us, bringing us a profound sense of peace and unwavering strength.

God's desire is to meet us in the quiet place of His love, where His transformative power is everlasting. I urge you to make a daily habit of meeting with Him and allowing His Word to speak to you. This simple act has the potential to revolutionize your life.

Those who wait on the Lord shall renew their strength;
they shall mount up with wings like eagles, they shall run
and not be weary, they shall walk and not faint.
(Isaiah 40:31 NKJV)

STUDY GUIDE

Matthew 5:45; John 16:33; Psalm 19:14;
Luke 10:38–42; Psalm 46:10

PERSONAL REFLECTION

1. How attentive are you to the Spirit of God when reading His Word or talking with Him in prayer?
2. Are you giving God your undivided attention when you pray?

WHAT IS PRAYER?

Prayer is simply a conversation between you and God. It doesn't have to be elaborate or long and drawn out; it needs only to be sincere. One prayer is not better than the other, but some prayers may be more sincere. Some people pray only when they are in extreme circumstances, while others pray because they have developed a life of prayer. Prayer is God's invitation for us to communicate with Him.

- **Practice**

  Developing a solid prayer life requires practice and discipline. And just as with anything else you put your heart into, you will reap the rewards.

- **Rest**

  Rest is the place where faith grows. Allow yourself in prayer to rest your head upon your heavenly Father's chest, just as John the disciple did, so you can hear His heartbeat of love for you.

- **Appointed**

  Choose an appointed time to meet with the Father daily while imagining yourself seated next to Him in heaven.

- **Yearn**

  Yearn for time with Him, and let Him become the passion of your heart. Allow yourself to fall head over heels in love with Jesus.

To develop a life of prayer, we must want it. To choose a life of prayer, we must desire a deeper relationship with the person of prayer, God the Father.

You will seek Me and find Me,
when you search for Me with all your heart.
(Jeremiah 29:13 NKJV)

STUDY GUIDE
1 Thessalonians 5:16–18; Matthew 11:28–30;
Psalm 55:17; Psalm 42:1; Ephesians 6:18

PERSONAL REFLECTION
1. Is God your 911 number only, or do you yearn to spend more time with God?
2. Ask the Holy Spirit to increase your desire for more of Him in your life.

POSTURE YOUR HEART

The human brain in its complex nature often finds itself entangled in the web of worldly distractions, pulling a person away from the true essence of life. These distractions are seemingly successful in draining us emotionally, physically, financially, and spiritually, holding no real value. Day after day we find ourselves trapped in this cycle, while our heavenly Father patiently awaits our return to Him, understanding the struggles we face.

In Luke 10:38–42 we read that Jesus and His disciples came to the village where Mary and Martha lived. While Mary sat at Jesus' feet, listening to what He was teaching, Martha was distracted by everything that needed to be done around the house, including the dinner she was preparing for Jesus and the disciples. Frustrated that her sister was not helping her, Martha said to Jesus, "It seems unfair that Mary sits here while I do all the work. Tell her to help me!" But Jesus told Martha, "You're worried and upset about many things. But there's only one thing you should concern yourself with, and Mary has discovered it. It will not be taken away from her."

Martha was so distracted by the things around her, thinking her focus was on Jesus because He was her guest, that she even interrupted Jesus while He was teaching. Although Martha treasured the person of Jesus, she seemed to prefer something other than what was *in* Jesus; therefore, the posture of her heart was not in the place where Jesus was. This did not keep Jesus from loving Martha, but it did keep Martha (because of her choice) from knowing the fullness of His love for her.

Therefore the Lord said: "In as much as these people draw near with their mouths and honor Me with their lips, But have removed their hearts far from Me, And their fear toward Me is taught by the commandment of men."
(Isaiah 29:13 NKJV)

This verse reminds us that true worship is not about outward actions or words, but about the condition of our hearts. It warns against the danger of empty rituals and superficial worship, emphasizing the importance of a genuine and heartfelt connection with God.

Mary could quiet her mind, spirit, and body to focus only on Jesus. She knew true worship was about sitting at His feet, quietly listening when others were rushing about. Mary knew that worshiping Him was about loving Him and accepting His love for her. Mary treasured what was in Jesus, and Jesus treasured the posture of Mary's heart.

Worshiping God is not about the physical location but about the state of our hearts. God, being a Spirit, yearns for sincere worshipers who adore Him in spirit and truth. This emphasis on sincerity in worship should inspire and motivate us to deepen our spiritual connection, knowing that our heartfelt devotion is what truly matters to Him.

With my whole heart I have sought You; oh, let me not wander from Your commandments! Your word I have hidden in my heart, that I might not sin against You.

(Psalm 119:10–11 NKJV)

STUDY GUIDE
Luke 10:38–42; John 4:23–24; John 3:23–24

PERSONAL REFLECTION

1. Where is your focus?
2. What is stopping you from allowing yourself to sit with Jesus and focus only on Him?

THE HEART OF PRAYER

Through many years of knowing Christ as my Lord and Savior, He has become my closest friend. He has always been faithful and has never let me down. Have my prayers always been answered? I have to say yes, in God's timing, not mine, and not always in the way I desired. But that doesn't mean He didn't hear and answer my prayers.

Prayer Requires Discipline.

We discipline our bodies to exercise, diet, play instruments, learn new languages, and so on. Likewise, we must develop a disciplined prayer life—because every relationship requires communication. And it's the same with God.

Bodily exercise profits a little, but godliness is profitable for all things, having promise of the life that now is and of that which is to come.
(1 Timothy 4:8 NKJV)

Prayer Requires Listening.

Most of us would rather talk than listen because talking is easier. Sometimes we need to be reminded to shut our mouths, open our ears, and quiet our minds. We often go into our prayer time and need to remember to listen. Being still does not mean you are simply sitting still. It means your spirit and your mind are still. I have learned to do this by retreating to a quiet place and focusing solely on Jesus.

How does God speak to you? Sometimes it is in a whisper or in a scripture; other times it is in the peace that He gives. But whatever you hear Him saying to you will always line up with His Word, the Bible, which is His love letter to you. Knowing the voice of God comes from a relationship with Him. He spoke in a whisper many times throughout the Bible. When He speaks in a whisper, it's not just a message but also an invitation to come closer, to be in His presence.

Draw near to God and He will draw near to you.

(James 4:8 NKJV)

What Is Prayer?

According to Wikipedia, the root word for *prayer* is derived from the Latin word *precari*, meaning "to beg." The Hebrew equivalent, *tefilah*, along with its root, *pelel,* means "the act of self-analysis or self-evaluation."

What if every time we prayed, we approached God with a humble heart of repentance that self-analyzes and evaluates?

God resists the proud, but gives grace to the humble.

(James 4:6 NKJV)

STUDY GUIDE
Galatians 6:9; John 13:23; Daniel 6:10; Ephesians 2:6;
Isaiah 26:9; Luke 18:10–14

PERSONAL REFLECTION
1. When you pray, is it with a heart of humble repentance?
2. Are you quieting your spirit to listen or are you doing
   most of the talking?

INTIMACY WITH GOD

When the disciples, eager to deepen their spiritual connection, asked Jesus how to pray, He redirected their focus from *how* to *who*. He urged them to direct their prayers to our Father in heaven, emphasizing the importance of relationship with God (Luke 11:1–4).

A great prayer life requires an authentic love relationship with God. Our prayer life should not be about our love for God but about realizing *His* immense love for *us* and that we are safe, secure, and at peace in His arms. Prayer is about intimacy with the Father in the quiet place where our souls are at rest, placing our cares upon His shoulders and knowing He cares for us. We no longer have to walk in a false identity of who we are or confusion about who He called us to be, because we are His and His alone.

We don't *have* to pray—we *get* to pray; and our prayer life should be intentional. If being alone with God the Father, Jesus the Son, and the person of the Holy Spirit is a foreign place for you, I encourage you to discipline yourself to sit alone with Him in seclusion until it becomes not what you do but rather is a part of who you are. When the passion of our hearts is to be with Him, our level of intimacy with Him will become more significant, and it will show in every part of our lives, inspiring hope and transformation.

Jesus had an intimate relationship with the Father, and His heart was constantly connected to and consumed by the Father.

Intimacy is our heart entwined with His, woven together with Him. After all, if God knit us together in our mother's wombs, was it not His desire to also incorporate His heart into ours?

What is intimacy, and how do you develop it?

* **Emotional Intimacy**

  Emotional intimacy is about feeling safe to share our deepest fears and dreams. We confide in those we trust and do not expect them to betray us. David set an example of this in the Psalms; he was continually pouring his deepest feelings out to God.

* **Intellectual Intimacy**

  Intellectual intimacy is having a two-way conversation with God. We are shown an example in Genesis 18:20–33, when the Lord told Abraham, "I have heard a great outcry against Sodom and Gomorrah because of their sin." Abraham asked God to spare the life of Lot and his family. Another example is in Exodus 32:30, when Moses prepared to ask God to spare the people who had sinned.

* **Experiential Intimacy**

  Remember where we have been and God's many blessings in our lives. Praise Him for what He has brought us through, and trust Him with the future. We read of David's experiential intimacy with God in 1 Samuel 17:37, when David stood before Goliath: "The Lord, who rescued me from the lion and the bear, will rescue me from the Philistine."

- **Spiritual Intimacy**
  Schedule a regular time to spend time with God. You don't
  have to work at it; just be yourself. We read in Daniel 6:10
  that Daniel prayed three times a day and gave thanks to the
  Lord.

The fear of intimacy because we may get hurt can overtake
us if we let it. But we will never feel safe until we are at rest in
the Father's arms. He knows our hearts and how we long to
be loved and accepted for who we are. He knows our longings
to discover His unique plan for our lives, which can be found
only as we spend time with Him—realizing His great love for
us, His children, His creation, His treasured jewels.

*Being confident of this very thing, that He who
has begun a good work in you will complete
it until the day of Jesus Christ.*

(Philippians 1:6 NKJV)

STUDY GUIDE

Matthew 6:9; 1 Peter 5:7; Psalm 82:6; Psalm 139:13–15;
Psalm 143:5; 1 Samuel 17:37; Daniel 6:10–28; Luke 2:42–49;
1 Samuel 17:32–37; Luke 2:42–49

PERSONAL REFLECTION

1. Have you allowed yourself to become intimate with God?
2. What steps can you take to draw closer to Him?

COME UP A LITTLE HIGHER

The most incredible privilege we will ever have on earth is communicating with the God of the universe. Prayer is an invitation to rise higher as you position your heart in the place of rest with the Father in heaven. There is no better place to be than seated next to Him. The privilege of prayer is not something to be taken lightly, but a gift that should fill us with gratitude and humility.

I am not a pilot, but from what I understand about flying, the plane engine must have full power to get off the ground. The higher a large aircraft flies, the less fuel it will use. When a small plane flies, it must go higher to get out of the dense fog unless it depends on the plane's navigation system.

After countless hours of prayer throughout the years, I have come to a profound realization. When I position my heart in the heavens while seated next to my heavenly Father, I use less fuel, just like a plane that flies higher. I am not worn out from the battle of spiritual warfare, even though it took the full power of determination to discipline myself to get there in mind, soul, and body. Thus, I have learned how to pray from heaven to earth rather than from earth to heaven. If we are seated with Him in heavenly places, it only stands to reason that we pray from the seated position of rest with the Father This transformative power of prayer is not just a concept, but a reality that can be experienced by each one of us.

While in prayer, I have often felt the Spirit of the Lord prompting me to come closer to Him. In those sacred moments, I hear Him say, "Come up a little higher. Sit with Me; learn of me. Allow Me to transform you into My image. Then, as you train yourself to be still in mind, soul, and body, I will unveil a new depth of My love for you and share the mysteries of My kingdom." This intimate connection with the divine is a journey we can all embark on.

When I asked a pilot friend of mine why he likes to fly, he said that climbing above the clouds into the blue sky on a dreary, cloudy day lifts his spirits and is very peaceful. He feels that it is very challenging and rewarding. Another pilot friend told me she could see for miles, and everything below seemed small. On a cloudy day, she said, you can see rainbows beneath the plane as if prisms were hanging from heaven.

When we come to Him in prayer while seated next to Him in heavenly places, it is then that we will begin hearing the heartbeat of the Father and speak the language of heaven. As we turn our gaze upon Jesus, we will view our challenges from a higher perspective, where they seem small, rising above the clouds on a dreary day to the peace and rest that only He can give so that others may see the glory of the Father shining through us.

"Come up here, and I will show you things which must take place."
(Revelation 4:1 NKJV)

As I soar like a bird to the heavens above
in touch with my Savior's grace, mercy, and love
He speaks in a whisper and allows me to hear
the heartbeat of heaven as He draws me near
What an honor to sit in His presence and rest
above cares and worries as I lean on His chest
While resting my feet on the things down below
I soar in the clouds, where His peace freely flows
—Kathleen VonSeggern

*"Our Father in heaven, hallowed be Your name. Your kingdom
come. Your will be done on earth as it is in heaven."*
(Matthew 6:9–10 NKJV)

STUDY GUIDE
Ephesians 2:6; Matthew 6:10; 1 Corinthians 2:10;
Proverbs 23:7; Psalm 23:5

PERSONAL REFLECTION
1. While praying, picture yourself seated at the table He has prepared for you, and leave your cares with Him.
2. Are you willing to change the way you think, allowing Christ to transform your life?

FROM HEAVEN TO EARTH

"Seek first the kingdom of God and His righteousness,
and all these things shall be added to you."
(Matthew 6:33 NKJV)

What is a kingdom? Webster tells us that a kingdom is a government, country, realm, domain, or territory headed by a king or queen. The spiritual realm of God is a kingdom. There is a constitution or a covenant between the king and the citizens. There are principles in which it functions.

In Philippians 1:27 and 3:17–20 we are not just told but invited to live as citizens of heaven (a kingdom). As citizens, we have a legal right to the keys of the realm of heaven.

"I will give you the keys of the kingdom of heaven, and
whatever you bind on earth will be bound in heaven, and
whatever you loose on earth will be loosed in heaven."
(Matthew 16:19 NKJV)

In this context, the "keys" represent the authority and power given to believers by God. They are not physical keys, but spiritual tools that allow us to access and operate in the kingdom of heaven's principles and power.

When Jesus taught His disciples to pray, I believe His heart desired them to pray from heaven to the earth rather than from earth to heaven. If Scripture tells us in Ephesians 2:6–7 that we are seated with Him in heavenly places, than why are we not praying from the place of rest with Him?

Most of us have spent our entire lives trying to defy gravity, because gravity causes items to go down, not up. We sometimes forget or have never realized that we are citizens of the kingdom of heaven. When we understand who we are, we will recognize what we have access to. Because as sons and daughters of God, we have access to everything in the Father's house.

The enemy doesn't come against what you're doing; he comes against who you are. One of his greatest fears is that you will realize your true identity as children of the King and begin to walk in it. But nothing is yours until you understand it.

So how do we start living and praying as citizens of a kingdom that we cannot see, a kingdom that we have only read about? The answer lies in our relationship with the Lord of the domain. We must first seek Him, not just for His benefits but for the depth of His love and wisdom.

You will seek Me and find Me,
when you search for Me with all your heart.
(Jeremiah 29:13 NKJV)

"Ask, and it will be given to you; seek,
and you will find; knock, and it will be opened to you."
(Matthew 7:7 NKJV)

STUDY GUIDE
Philippians 1:27; 3:17–20; Matthew 16:19;
Ephesians 2:6–7

PERSONAL REFLECTION
1. Are you seeking the kingdom of heaven above all else?
2. Ask the Holy Spirit to reveal to you a greater revelation of your citizenship in the kingdom of God. Journal your thoughts.

JESUS, OUR EXAMPLE

He Himself often withdrew into the wilderness and prayed.
(Luke 5:16 NKJV)

The key word in Luke 5:16 is *often*. Jesus Himself showed us not only how we should live but also what a life of prayer looks like. Below I have only begun to touch on the many times we are told that Jesus prayed:

- When the Holy Spirit descended upon Him: *Luke 3:21-22*
- All night before choosing who would be His twelve disciples: *Luke 6:12–17*
- Before feeding the five thousand families with five loaves of bread and two fish: *Matthew 14:17–21*
- Jesus was alone with His disciples praying just before asking them if they had a clear revelation of who He was: *Luke 9:18–22*
- Just before the disciples came to Him and asked Him to teach them how to pray: *Luke 11:1–4*
- At Lazarus' tomb: *John 11:38–44*
- Before Judas betrayed Him: *John 17:1—18:9*
- He prayed earnestly in Gethsemane to the point of sweating drops of blood: *Luke 22:44*
- On the cross for others: *Luke 23:33–46*

Jesus was full of and led by the Holy Spirit because He spent time with the person of the Holy Spirit. If time alone with God was essential for Jesus, should it not be essential in our lives too?

When all the people were baptized, it came to pass that Jesus also was baptized; and while He prayed, the heaven was opened. And the Holy Spirit descended in bodily form like a dove upon Him, and a voice came from heaven which said, "You are My beloved Son; in You I am well pleased."

(Luke 3:21 NKJV)

STUDY GUIDE

Luke 3:21–22; Luke 6:12–17; Mark 6:35–44; Luke 9:18–22;
Luke 9:28–36; Luke 11:1–4; John 11:40–44; Matthew 26:26;
Luke 22:39–44; Luke 23:34, 46; Luke 24:30–31;
1 Thessalonians 5:16–18; Matthew 14:17–21; John 17:1—18:9

PERSONAL REFLECTION

1. What does your prayer life look like?
2. In what ways could the time you spend with God become the highlight of your day?

LIFE APPLICATION

Thank you, Heavenly Father, for the invitation to communicate with you. What an honor and privilege it is to be able to spend time with you! I ask that the gems hidden within the Bible would sparkle, becoming more evident as I seek out the treasure hidden within your Word and that I will become more aware of the treasure I am to you. Help me to position my heart in the place of rest with you to hear your voice. Teach me how to be still, knowing that you are God. Forgive me for not standing against the injustice of this world in prayer. I ask you to guide and direct me in the choices I make and that the words of my mouth and meditation of my heart will be acceptable to you.

In your name I pray.

Amen

3

FAITH

Facing the Unknown with Confidence

FAITH: INTRODUCTION

A gem of faith as small as a mustard seed possesses the transformative power of God's kingdom to the earth, making the impossible possible. We have each been given a measure of faith from God's treasure chest in heaven. But just as a seed must be nurtured to grow, our faith too needs to be supplemented with treasures found in the Word of God and a relationship with the Holy Spirit.

I have found that God has always met me there when I use my mustard seed of faith and step out of my comfort zone. He has remained faithful no matter what the situation. And because of His faithfulness and love for me, my faith has grown from a mustard seed to strong roots established deep within my soul.

Years ago the Lord prompted me to join a local secular public speaking group. The Lord told me that His future plans would be much easier for me if I participated in this group. So

I stepped out of my comfort zone in faith, trusting the Lord each step of the way. It took work! Each week I prepared a speech to share. And with my fingernails digging deeply into the flooring, I dragged myself in front of a group of people to speak. I did this each week for a year. Within that year several speaking opportunities opened up in areas unrelated to the group. Several years later I felt the prompting of the Lord to start a blog, which soon became a website and a small ministry. Again, it's not my comfort zone. Yet by the grace of God I have found myself ministering through technology to countless people in parts of the world I have never traveled. As inadequate as I feel, I trust His Spirit within me. And I know that whatever the journey involves, God is faithful.

He who calls you is faithful.
(1 Thessalonians 5:24 NLT)

As you read this chapter, I pray that your desire to supplement your faith with the Word of God and the time spent with the person of the Holy Spirit will increase so you'll see His kingdom come on earth just as it is in heaven, as His plans for your life unfold in a way you never expected.

BROKEN DREAMS

God has placed dreams within each of our hearts. One person's dream is no more important than that of another. Your dream is your dream—don't let anyone or anything destroy the dream within your heart. The fulfillment of some dreams may take longer than others, thus involving a lot of detours along the way. But no matter the journey, a dream fulfilled is satisfying to the soul. The stepping stones along the way always serve a purpose, and we must not despise small beginnings, having faith that He is a God of His word. In the meantime, while we wait for our dreams to be fulfilled, let us focus on growing in our faith, serving others, and trusting in God's plan for our lives.

*Hope deferred makes the heart sick, but when
the desire comes, it is a tree of life.*
(Proverbs 13:12 NKJV)

- **Caleb waited forty-five years to receive the land promised to him.**
  Caleb was forty years old when Moses sent him to explore the land of Canaan. He was eighty-five years old before he received the land promised to him (see *Joshua 14:6–15).*

- **David waited fourteen years to become king.**
  David was a teenager when Samuel anointed him to be king. He became king when he was thirty (see *1 Samuel 16:13; 2 Samuel 5:4–5*).

- **Joseph waited thirteen years for his dream to come to pass.**
  Joseph shared a dream with his brothers when he was seventeen. He was thirty years old when his dream came to pass (see *Genesis 37:2—50:26*).

- **Abraham waited twenty-five years for a son.**
  Abraham was seventy-five years old when he received word that he would be the father of many nations. He was one hundred years old when Issac was born (see *Genesis 17:1—21:7*).

Even though the Bible gives us examples of fulfilled dreams of the human heart, we may sometimes feel God has forgotten us. But remember: the patience and faith of these biblical figures were tested, yet they persevered. God is fully aware of the dreams within your heart and what is written in His Word concerning you.

He has made everything beautiful in its time.
(Ecclesiastes 3:11 NKJV)

Trust in God's timing, for He knows the perfect moment to bring your dream to fruition. Your dream is not delayed; it's being beautifully prepared for you.

STUDY GUIDE

Joshua 14:6–15; 2 Samuel 5:4–5; Genesis 37:2—50:26;
Genesis 17:1–25; Genesis 21:1–7; Matthew 7:7–11

PERSONAL REFLECTION

1. What is the dream in your heart?
2. Are you willing to wait for God's timing for it to be fulfilled?

STEP OUT OF THE BOAT

In Matthew 14:22–33 we read about a storm that arose in the darkness of night, causing the boat the disciples were in to be tossed and battered by the wind and waves. During the fourth night watch (between 3 a.m. and 6 a.m.), Jesus went out to them, walking on the water. When the disciples saw Him, they were terrified because they thought He was a ghost. But Jesus immediately said to them, "It is I; do not be afraid."

Then Peter called to Him, "Lord, if it's you, tell me to come to you on the water."

"Come," Jesus said.

So Peter stepped out of the boat and walked toward Jesus on the water. But when he saw the wind and waves, fear began overtaking him, and he began sinking, crying out to Jesus to save him. Immediately Jesus reached out His hand and caught Peter. "You of little faith, why did you doubt?" He said.

Peter's decision to step out of the boat and walk on water toward Jesus was a testament to his unwavering trust in Jesus. He wanted to emulate Jesus, to do what Jesus was doing. This act of courage, of fixing his eyes on the author and finisher of his faith, allowed Peter to defy the laws of nature. As long as Peter kept his eyes on Jesus, he could walk on top of the water. But when he took his eyes off Jesus, fear crept in and he began sinking.

When I think of Peter walking on the water, I like to think of the water representing the circumstances of life, which at times can overtake us, just like the water surrounded Peter. But keeping our focus on Jesus and trusting Him amidst whatever we are going through can enable us to walk above the circumstances of life that surround us—knowing that whatever life brings, God is bigger and His plan is perfect.

When life hits us out of nowhere and is hard to understand, it's easy to become immersed in the circumstances surrounding us. But as we fix our eyes on Jesus, we can walk above the circumstances in faith. Even though the storm around us is still raging, the storm within us will be at peace.

No temptation has overtaken you except such as is common to man; but God is faithful, who will not allow you to be tempted beyond what you are able, but with the temptation will also make the way of escape, that you may be able to bear it.

(1 Corinthians 10:13 NKJV)

STUDY GUIDE
Matthew 14:22–23; Psalm 16:8

PERSONAL REFLECTION

1. Do you feel as if you are drowning in the circumstances of life?
2. What might happen if you focus on Jesus instead of your problems?

UNCHARTED TERRITORY

It is always exciting and fun to vacation somewhere we've never been. We prepare for the journey with just the right clothes and an agenda to make our trip a wonderful experience.

But what about the uncharted territory that life brings that we never planned? Life can be full of surprises; some are pleasant and others are not. During tough times we may learn and grow or stumble aimlessly, wondering what brought us to this place, thus creating a vicious circle where the path is different but the journey is the same.

We read in Genesis 12:1–9 about Abraham, who trusted God to lead and guide him on an unknown journey. Although Abraham could have chosen to stay with his family and friends in the land he had become accustomed to, he decided to obey God. Abraham was seventy-five years old when he left his homeland to step out on a journey in which the only road map he had was the instruction from God along the way. Notice that God told Abraham, "Go to the land I will show you." Abraham did not know what lay ahead of him on this new journey. He only knew that he had to listen for instruction along the way. Even though there were times when Abraham messed up, God was always faithful. He had an incredible plan for Abraham's life, even though by this time Abraham was seventy-five years old.

I have found myself in uncharted territory more times than I can count. Sometimes it was stressful, and I felt anxious and afraid because I couldn't see the road map. Then God in His mercy and grace gently reminded me not to seek His *hand* (what He could do for me) but to seek His *face* (who He is).

In that place I began trusting God again with His plan for my life, knowing that there is no uncharted territory in Him, only plans for a future and hope.

We live by believing and not by seeing.

(2 Corinthians 5:7 NLT)

STUDY GUIDE
Genesis 12:1–9; Jeremiah 29:11

PERSONAL REFLECTION

1. Describe your journey of faith.
2. Is trusting God difficult for you? Why?

A PURPOSE-DRIVEN WOMAN

In Luke 8:43–48 we read of a woman who, after living in isolation for twelve years with a continual bleeding issue in faith, pushed her way through a crowd surrounding Jesus. Trying to remain unnoticed, she reached out to touch the hem of His garment—and instantly she was healed! Among the crowd's noise she heard a voice asking, "Who touched me?" When she realized she could no longer remain unnoticed, the woman fell trembling at Jesus' feet and in front of the crowd declared, "I was desperate to touch you, Jesus—because I knew that if I could touch only the hem of your garment, my life would never be the same." Jesus was moved with compassion and said to her, "Beloved daughter, your faith has made you well. Go in peace."

Despite knowing she was considered unclean and that being near others was forbidden in her condition, this woman was determined to get to Jesus. She had spent everything she had on doctors, and Jesus was her last hope. When no one else would touch her or have anything to do with her, Jesus revealed to the crowd that she had touched Him. He acknowledged her as His beloved daughter, and because of her faith, she was healed. Jesus could have kept silent, knowing that healing had gone out of Him. But He wanted her to come forward and confess her faith in Him publicly. Additionally, He wanted to make public that she was accepted, loved, and healed by Him. In doing this, she experienced not only physical healing but emotional and spiritual healing as well.

We live in a world where people have lost hope as they continue suffering and bleeding from past hurts, anxiety, and fear. As a result, they isolate themselves, fearing rejection.

Just as the woman with the issue of blood, you may have sought answers and tried everything, only to be disappointed and lose hope. But regardless of the mountain you face today, regardless of the issue of blood, remember—God is bigger! Place your faith in Him and open your heart. As you reach out to Him in faith, He will meet you there.

"Seek first the kingdom of God, and His righteousness, and all these things shall be added to you."

(Matthew 6:33 NKJV)

STUDY GUIDE
Luke 8:43–48; Hebrews 11:6

PERSONAL REFLECTION

1. Have you been desperate to be where Jesus is?
2. What are you willing to do to get to Jesus? Journal your thoughts.

UNLIKELY PEOPLE

---

*Now faith is the substance of things hoped for, the evidence
of things not seen. For by it the elders obtained a
good testimony. By faith we understand that the worlds
were framed by the word of God, so that the things which
are seen were not made of things which are visible.*

(Hebrews 11:1–3 NKJV)

Life is a journey; some parts are good, and some are bad,
but wherever that journey takes us, the most important thing
is that we learn and grow through the process. Life's journey
has been a roller coaster for me with my seat belt securely
fastened in my faith and trust in God. Through it all, God
has proven Himself faithful and has never let me down.
Sometimes I doubted, became discouraged, felt like giving up,
and was lonely. But God has been my refuge, my constant help
in trouble, and He remains true to this day!

I often think of some of the most unlikely people to be
used by God:

- **Saul (Paul)** hunted down and murdered Christians, yet
  God chose him: *Acts 9*
- **Abraham** was too old to become the father of many nations.
  Nevertheless, his son Isaac was born when Abraham was
  one hundred years old: *Genesis 17:4; 21:5*
- **Moses** beat a man to death and hid the body in the sand,
  yet God chose him to lead the Hebrews to freedom: *Exodus*

2:11–12; 3:1–22
- **Rahab** was a prostitute, yet the lineage of Jesus came from her: *Joshua 2; Matthew 1:5*
- **Jeremiah** thought himself too young to be a prophet, but God chose him anyway: *Jeremiah 1:7*
- **Peter and John** were unschooled, ordinary men, but they boldly proclaimed Jesus after being filled with the Holy Spirit at Pentecost: *Acts 4:13–20*

Life is not fair, and people are not perfect. Nevertheless, we each must walk out our own journey. Whoever you are or wherever you've been, God has a plan and a purpose for your life. We must remember that the only one the Bible ever referred to as perfect was Jesus.

Stepping out into the unknown can be challenging. We can all relate to those in the Bible who felt inadequate and unqualified. But in that place, we become entirely dependent on God, and He gets all the glory and praise.

Just step out in faith and keep your focus on Him.

I can do all things though Christ who strengthens me.
(Philippians 4:13 NKJV)

STUDY GUIDE

Acts 9; Genesis 17:4; Genesis 21:5; Exodus 2:11–12;
Exodus 3:1–22; Exodus 4:10; Joshua 2; Matthew 1:5;
Jeremiah 1:7; Acts 4:13–20; 2 Corinthians 12:9–10

PERSONAL REFLECTION

1. In what ways have you felt inadequate?
2. In what ways have you depended on your own ability?

THROUGH THE ROOF

In Mark 2:1–12 we read about four friends, passionate about seeing their mutual friend healed, working together to get him to Jesus. These four men wanted their paralyzed friend healed so desperately that they were willing to carry him on a sleeping mat to Capernaum, where Jesus was. How far they took him we do not know. It may have been miles. They may have had to carry him through muck and mire or in the heat of the day. But whatever the obstacles along the way, they were determined to work together to get to where Jesus was.

When the men arrived at the house where Jesus was teaching, they found Him surrounded by a crowd of people. Driven by their faith in Jesus and determination to finish what they had set out to do, the men decided to lower their friend on the mat in front of Jesus through the roof. We do not know how high the house's roof was or if these men had to build or find a ladder. But we do know that these men had to work together, strategically in unity, to carry their friend on his sleeping mat to the roof of the house and then remove the roof tiles so that they could lower him in front of Jesus.

What great faith these four men must have had to go to such lengths with love and passion to see their friend healed! They stopped at nothing because they knew that Jesus was the only one who could genuinely make a difference in his life, assured that Jesus could and would heal their friend. I imagine they knew the sound and frequency of Jesus' voice because they had been with Him where He was. Therefore, they had no problem climbing a little higher to lower their friend to the exact spot where Jesus was standing.

How often have we failed to realize God's love and grace for us and the price He paid so that we could be set free? How often have we stopped short of pursuing our journey with Him because of the muck and the mire or the rude, pushy crowd? How often have we fallen short because of the heavy load and work it took to carry our friends or needs to Jesus? And as if that weren't enough of a journey, we still had to climb higher and remove some roof tiles while listening for the sound of His voice amidst our busy lives.

Faith comes by hearing, and hearing by the word of God.
(Romans 10:17 NKJV)

STUDY GUIDE
Mark 2:1–11; Romans 10:17; Psalm 103:2–5

PERSONAL REFLECTION

1. What have you given up on because of the obstacles in your way?
2. Are you willing to go the extra mile to bring your friends to Jesus?

THE DARKEST HOUR

When the storm clouds hover over us day after day, never seeming to pass, and the darkness around us seems to close in, making life uncomfortable, it can be overwhelming. We do not often think of darkness as a place where God dwells. But if He resides in you and you are in that place in your life, He's right there with you, offering His comforting presence.

"The Lord, He is the One who goes before you.
He will be with you, He will not leave you nor
forsake you; do not fear nor be dismayed."
(Deuteronomy 31:8 NKJV)

Before digital technology, cameras that contained film were used to take pictures. The film had to be taken into a dark room and cut into separate pieces, called negatives. Photographers worked carefully to develop the film using chemicals, ensuring that they did not ruin the pictures during development.

Have you ever considered that dark place in your life as the place where God is developing a godly character within you? He desires not only to grow our character in the dark places of our lives but also for us to seek Him in the good and bad times.

David was anointed by God twenty-two years before he became the king. His character developed in the hidden places of a field, practicing with a sling, killing lions and bears while watching over sheep, and later in a cave when running and hiding for his life (see 1 Samuel 16:11—2 Samuel 5).

Joseph was in a deep, dark hole in the ground and later in prison, serving time for a crime he hadn't committed. Yet during this time he was being developed with the character he needed for the high position God had ordained for him (see Genesis 37–50).

We must trust God even in the hard times, allowing Him to hold us when we have no more strength left. We must know that His plan for our lives will come forth as His character is developed in us.

"These things I have spoken to you, that in Me you may have peace. In the world you will have tribulation; but be of good cheer, I have overcome the world."

(John 16:33 NKJV)

STUDY GUIDE

1 Samuel 16:11—2 Samuel 5; Genesis 37–50; Isaiah 45:3

PERSONAL REFLECTION

1. In what ways has your character been developed during the darkest times of your life?
2. Or—do you find yourself routinely experiencing the same problems?

GOD IS BIGGER

Life isn't easy, and there may be times when we feel that it's hard to trust a God we cannot see. Or perhaps we feel as if He has given up on us because we have given up on Him. But when we are in the depths of the water, feeling as though we may drown, or walking around in the desert where nothing ever grows, we must remember that He is the God of the impossible—and that's where He does His best work! God promised never to leave or forsake us.

Although it looked as if . . .

- . . . the Israelites would die at the hand of the Egyptians or drown in the Red Sea—God parted the sea, and they walked across on dry ground! Then God said to Moses, "Raise your staff and stretch out your hand over the sea to divide the water so the Israelites can go through on the dry ground": *Exodus 14:21–31*

- . . . three young Hebrew men would burn in a furnace—at the king's command, Shadrach, Meshach, and Abednego, fully clothed and firmly tied, were thrown into a blazing furnace. Because of the king's anger, the furnace was turned up seven times hotter than usual. But when the king looked into the furnace, he saw not three but four unbound and unharmed men walking around. And the fourth looked like the Son of God. When the men came out of the furnace, not a hair on their head was singed. Their robes were not scorched, and there was not even the smell of smoke on them: *Daniel 3:19–27*

- . . . all hope for Lazarus was gone, since he was now dead—Jesus with authority called him to come out of the grave. Lazarus, still wrapped in grave clothes, came out of the tomb, and Jesus said to them, "Unwrap him": *John 11:1–44*

- . . . Jesus was never coming back, since He was now dead—on the first day of the week, very early in the morning, some women came to the tomb bringing the spices that they had prepared for Jesus' body. Finding the stone rolled away, they entered the tomb—where Jesus was *not* found. Instead, two men stood by them in shining garments and said to them, "The one you seek is not dead. He is alive and has risen!": *Luke 24:1–6*

There is no mountain too high, no journey too long, and no valley too deep that the prayer of faith in God cannot help you through it! You may be at a point where you feel a flood of sorrow and heartache will overtake you. But God is bigger than your broken heart, broken dreams, or broken body. In Him there is hope.

Jesus Christ is the same yesterday, today, and forever.
(Hebrews 13:8 NKJV)

STUDY GUIDE

Mark 10:27; Exodus 14:21–31; Daniel 3:19–27;
John 11:1–44; Luke 24:1–6

PERSONAL REFLECTION

1. In what ways have you lost hope?
2. Can you think of a time when a miracle happened in your life? Journal your thoughts.

A RAM IN THE THICKET

In Genesis 22:9–13 we read that God told Abraham to take his only son, Isaac, whom he loved, and sacrifice him as a burnt offering on the mountain. Early the next morning Abraham saddled his donkey and took two servants, along with his son, Isaac. He chopped wood for a fire and set out for the place where God had instructed him to go. On the third day of their journey Abraham saw the area in the distance. Speaking in faith to his servants, Abraham told them to wait with the donkey while he and the boy traveled a little farther to worship, and then they would return. Notice that Abraham spoke in faith when he said that he and his son would return. When Isaac asked Abraham where the sheep were for the burnt offering, Abraham told Isaac that God would provide a sheep for the offering.

Then Abraham lifted his eyes and looked, and there behind him was a ram caught in a thicket by its horns.
(Genesis 22:13 NKJV)

Years before, God had made a covenant with Abraham that he would be the father of many nations, but Abraham's total obedience and faith were tested before God's promise could be fulfilled.

We all have things in our lives that we cling to, but God yearns to fill every corner of our hearts. As you release your grip on whatever you've been holding onto, God will always provide a solution, just as he did for Abraham with the ram caught in the thicket.

Trust in the Lord with all your heart;
do not depend on your own understanding.

(Proverbs 3:5 NLT)

STUDY GUIDE
Genesis 22:1–9; Hebrews 11:17

PERSONAL REFLECTION
1. What or who is the "Isaac" in your life?
2. Are you willing to trust God with the treasure of your heart?

HEAVEN'S ARMY

Trials—we all have them. No matter who we are, none of us is immune. Trials can cause all kinds of emotions, such as fear, anxiety, regret, pity, and depression. But how can we change the way we look at things and how we come out on the other side?

Scripture tells us in 1 Peter 5:6–7 to cast all our cares on God because He cares for us. While this may seem challenging, it's essential to understand that God's love and care for us are unwavering. He is always there, ready to shoulder our burdens and guide us through our trials.

We read in 2 Kings 6:13–17 that a king sent horses, chariots, and a strong army at night to surround the city where Elisha and his assistant were staying. When the assistant got up and went out early the following day, an army with horses and chariots had surrounded the city. "Oh, my Lord—what shall we do?" the assistant asked.

"Don't be afraid," Elisha answered. "There are more with us than with them." Then Elisha prayed for the Lord to open his assistants' eyes so he could see. The Lord opened his eyes, and he saw the hills full of horses and chariots of fire all around.

We are to remember those who have gone before us in the faith, consider the outcome of their way of life, and imitate their faith. If Jesus Christ is the same yesterday, today, and forever, then is not the God of Elisha the same God we serve today? Is Elisha not one of the leaders we must remember and imitate his faith?

There are angels all around us. So when we think about an army of angels around us ready to fight for us, what do we have to fear? Because if God is for us, then who can possibly be against us?

I pray as you read this that your eyes will be opened and your heart will receive God's love for you. We need not fear— because our names are engraved on God's hand, so He can never forget us. The scars on His hands are always before His eyes as a reminder of His love for us.

We can stand in faith knowing that the same God who created the universe knew us before we were formed in our mother's womb, and He has a plan for our life. The God of Elisha is still God today.

"Consider the rock from which you were cut, the quarry from which you were mined."

(Isaiah 51:1 NLT)

STUDY GUIDE

1 Peter 5:7; 2 Kings 6:13–17; Hebrews 13:7; Psalm 91:11–12;
Romans 8:31; Jeremiah 1:5; Matthew 16:17–19;
Psalm 91:9–13

PERSONAL REFLECTION

1. When facing a battle in life, are you looking through the eyes of faith or the eyes of fear?
2. Why is faith over fear important?

LIFE APPLICATION

Heavenly Father,

Thank you for the beautiful gem of a mustard seed of faith you have given each of us. I thank you for allowing us to supplement our faith and watch it grow as we glean from the treasure of your Word and develop a closer relationship with you. May each person reading this today be encouraged to step out in faith in whatever you have called him or her to do. I come against all fear and intimidation in the name of Jesus. I speak to those passions and desires lying dormant within each heart, and I say, "Arise in the name of Jesus."

Amen

4
OFFENSE

It's a Choice

OFFENSE: INTRODUCTION

The smell of smoke can be a sweet-smelling incense lingering in the air—or a stench from the fires we have battled throughout life.

It has often been said, "You can't take it with you." But discovering the treasure of forgiveness is one of the most significant gems you *will* carry to heaven.

We get hurt and often don't know how to deal with it. Broken people living in a broken world can produce only broken pieces. Not all wounds are the same or heal the same. And forgiveness is a process.

We take offense, and without knowing it, our hurt turns to anger, bitterness, and over time, a hardened heart. A hardened heart will change everything about us, such as how we live, treat people, and make decisions.

Forgiveness is a choice; it doesn't come easy but with a price. After years of physical, mental, emotional, and spiritual abuse, I placed a shield around my heart, determined that no one was ever going to hurt me again. I found myself living in fear of rejection. Everyone I met was a suspect of one who would forsake me. As I dealt with feeling alone and abandoned, God became my refuge. Yet after the loss of my second child due to miscarriage, I felt as though He too had abandoned me. I became angry at God. I was offended because He had not fulfilled my desire to have a child in the way that I longed for. Years later, after the live birth of my daughter, I became pregnant again. At five and a half months into my pregnancy, I gave birth to a stillborn child. At one of the lowest times of my life, I felt Jesus' presence in a way I had never felt before. I felt Him lying next to me on the bed, taking my pain. With His arms around me, holding me close to His chest, and amid despair, He met me there with a love that only He can give. At that moment I became captivated by His love for me again. My offense toward God was great, but not so great that His love and grace could not find me.

The process of forgiveness can be challenging. And no one deserves to be forgiven. Yet Jesus felt we were worth giving His life for. The fires we have battled may have left us smelling of smoke. He hung on the cross and paid the price so we could be free.

Let's discover the treasure of forgiveness together as we mine the gems hidden within God's Word to set the captives free.

*Let all bitterness, wrath, anger, clamor, and evil
speaking be put away from you, with all malice. And be
kind to one another, tenderhearted, forgiving one
another, even as God in Christ forgave you.*

(Ephesians 4:31–32 NKJV)

CHECK YOUR BAGGAGE

Traveling can be fun, but packing and preparing can require a lot of work, time, and energy. Traveling on a plane can get us where we are going faster, but we must ensure that what we pack or carry on with us agrees with the airline's federal regulations. Although it may cost less to carry a small bag, it may be more convenient to check the bag at the ticket counter.

What about the baggage we carry through life, baggage from past hurts, relationships, spoken words, and choices made by us or others—the stuff we carry that has cost us relationships, advancement, and blessings in our life? It's challenging to walk into the future when we load ourselves down with the baggage of the past. Rejection, bitterness, regret, offense, and unworthiness harm us and others. We need to check them at the gate of heaven.

How many times have we hidden among the baggage of our past because we were afraid of failure or of what others would say or think? We hide among the baggage we carry because we have yet to check the bags at heaven's gate. How much of it keeps us from moving forward into what God has for us? The favor of God comes when we move into a new season, allowing God to take the baggage of our past and give us a new heart.

"I will give you a new heart and put a new spirit within you; I will take the heart of stone out of your flesh and give you a heart of flesh."
(Ezekiel 36:26 NKJV)

Do not allow fear to hinder your progress toward the path God has planned for you. Instead, surrender to God's teachings and allow Him to shape you into the person He envisions. Let Him mend your heart, freeing you from the burden of past baggage.

If you aren't sure how to check at heaven's gate the baggage you've been carrying, you can talk to God just as you talk to the person next to you (because He's right next to you). Begin by telling Him what's on your heart and how you feel. Then give Him all the stuff that has been weighing you down.

Ask him to heal your heart and make it new. Then find someone to help lead and guide you through the Word of God. (Your local church may be able to help you with this.)

Casting all your care upon Him, for He cares for you.
(1 Peter 5:7 NKJV)

STUDY GUIDE

1 Samuel 10:17–27; John 1:12; Malachi 3:17;
Jeremiah 29:11; John 3:17

PERSONAL REFLECTION

1. What baggage from your past are you still carrying?
2. What is stopping you from checking your baggage at heaven's gate?

THE BELT OF TRUTH

I believe some of the best advice given was from a pastor whose last dying words to his family were "Always be humble, be gentle, and do not take offense." Since I heard this advice, it has become a part of my daily prayer and has changed my life.

Paul encourages us in Ephesians 6:10–17 to put on God's whole armor, which is freely provided for us throughout Scripture. Being humble, gentle, and not taking offense can be done only when we dress for battle in the whole armor of God, because it protects us from the struggles we face. Paul associates a soldier's belt with truth because God's Word is truth and is the foundation of our faith. In Jesus' day Roman soldiers stored their weapons close to their bodies in their belts.

However, some of us wear belts around our waists made up of lies rather than truth. We have wrapped offense around our waists and carry it wherever we go, even to bed at night. We wear it like a fanny pack to hide under our clothes. It is easily accessible and has lots of storage space to add more content. Even though it is heavy and may cause pain, we refuse to let it go because we feel it has value. After all, what has caused us to take offense is valid, and we carry it for protection. Therefore, we are building a wall of protection around our hearts toward everyone we meet.

When we allow an offense to occupy our hearts, we create a breeding ground for the negative seed sown. These offenses can be anything that causes us to feel hurt, angry, or resentful, such as a harsh word, a betrayal, or a misunderstanding. Thus, we cultivate an environment that is neither healthy nor Christ-like. Because out of offense come pride, rejection, insecurity, fear, and anger.

When we focus on the firm foundation of God's Word and nurture it daily, we break free from the chains that once held us captive. We no longer find solace in things that steal our peace, joy, and acceptance of others.

Jesus had more reason to take offense than anyone. Yet He replicated the heart of the Father. As Jesus was being nailed to the cross, He said, "Forgive them, Father, because they don't know what they're doing." And with a heart of understanding, compassion, and love, He paid the price for all offenses so that we don't have to live there anymore.

Always be humble and gentle. Be patient with each other, making allowance for each other's faults because of your love.

(Ephesians 4:2 NLT)

STUDY GUIDE

Ephesians 4:11–18; Ephesians 6:10–18;
Matthew 23:33–34; Matthew 7:24–27

PERSONAL REFLECTION

1. Ask the Holy Spirit to reveal the lies you have come to believe. Journal your thoughts.
2. Make it your daily prayer to always be humble, gentle, and not to take offense.

TAKING OFFENSE IS A CHOICE

What we have not let go of is still held captive in our hearts. If we are camping out where we were hurt, refusing to let go, the offense has taken up residence in our hearts.

If we know that God will take care of what we give Him, then why do we hold on so tightly to the wrongs others have done to us? Taking offense is a form of insecurity and pride, and when we allow ourselves to become offended, our ability to hear the voice of God becomes less accurate.

"I have blotted out, like a thick cloud,
your transgressions, and like a cloud, your sins.
Return to Me, for I have redeemed you."
(Isaiah 44:22 NKJV)

When we allow an offense to take root, forgiving becomes more difficult. But when we choose to forgive sooner rather than later, we avoid the root of bitterness. Biblical forgiveness is not a feeling. It's a choice we make. Scripture reminds us of those who chose to take offense and those who decided to forgive. Let's look at a few:

- If Daniel had entered the lion's den with offense in his heart instead of peace and forgiveness, those lions would have enjoyed a tasty meal that night: *Daniel 6:22*
- Saul never knew his identity or who God created him to be, so he was offended by David's mere existence.

Moreover, Saul feared that David would one day be seated on his throne. And for many years he tried to kill David. Thus, the very thing he feared came to pass. And when Saul died, David became king: *1 Samuel 19—2 Samuel 2:1-4*

- David knew his God-given identity and lived confidently in it. David could have taken offense at Saul's hatred toward him. But instead, he chose to forgive and honor Saul even to death. Because he feared God more than man, David continued showing Saul honor and respect: *1 Samuel 24:1-13*

- The last miracle Jesus ever did before going to the cross was to heal the ear of the soldier who came to arrest Him. If Jesus had gone to the cross with offense in His heart, we would have had no hope of being set free: *Luke 22:50-51*

According to studies at Johns Hopkins, people who hang on to grudges are more likely to experience severe depression, post-traumatic stress disorder, and other health conditions. Forgiveness, however, calms stress levels, leading to improved health.

Sensible people control their temper;
they earn respect by overlooking wrongs.
(Proverbs 19:11 NLT)

STUDY GUIDE

2 Timothy 1:12; Daniel 6; 1 Samuel 18:5–16;
1 Samuel 19—2 Samuel 2:1–4; 1 Samuel 24;
John 18:10–11; Mark 11:25–26

PERSONAL REFLECTION

1. What does forgiveness look like to you?
2. Have you allowed offense to take up residence in your heart? Journal your thoughts.

A DIP IN THE RIVER

In 2 Kings 5:1–14 we read of a man named Naaman, a highly respected commander of the army of the king of Aram who suffered from leprosy. One day a servant girl who had been captured from Israel by the Arameans told Naaman's wife about a prophet in Samaria who could cure Naaman. Naaman arrived in Israel after receiving permission from the king of Aram to see the prophet, bearing gifts of silver and gold and a letter to the king of Israel. Standing outside the door of Elisha's house with his horses and chariots, Naaman expected the prophet to come out and meet him. But instead, Elisha sent a messenger to tell Naaman to dip seven times in the Jordan River, and God would heal him. But Naaman, offended and angry, stormed away because Elisha would not even come out of the house to meet him and had instructed him to dip seven times in a muddy river. After all, there were much cleaner rivers that Naaman could have dipped in. This wasn't comfortable for a man of honor like him and in front of the men he commanded. Naaman's pride caused him to take offense at the man of God. Had it not been for the reasoning and faith of the men in his army, Naaman's prideful anger may have kept him from being healed of leprosy.

How many times have we thought more highly of ourselves than we should? We become offended by others because of our pride, and we walk away from God's blessing. No matter what we have accomplished in life, God draws close to those who are humble and are willing to obey His voice. No matter how foolish it seems, God is more interested in the position of our hearts than the positions we hold.

Offense is a product of selfish pride and can be a barrier to God's blessings. If left unaddressed, it can build a defensive wall so strong that it may take years to dismantle. However, if we choose humility over offense, as Naaman eventually did, we open ourselves to God's blessings. This choice is crucial, as it can determine whether we receive God's favor or not.

Pride goes before destruction, and haughtiness before a fall.

(Proverbs 16:18 NLT)

STUDY GUIDE

2 Kings 5:1–14; Matthew 18:2–3

PERSONAL REFLECTION

1. Do you have a problem with pride and anger?
2. Can you think of a time when pride caused you to walk away from God's blessings?

THE MOUTH OF THE LION

We've all heard the saying "Sticks and stones may break my bones, but words can never harm me." But the truth is that words can indeed be very harmful. They can be like a lion waiting to devour those around it.

Words are powerful—they will speak either life or death. Unfortunately, in today's society cyberbullying and harassment have become increasingly common, especially among teenagers; this can include posting rumors and harmful remarks about a person.

Gossip is everywhere, and getting caught up in it is easy. The Bible speaks very clearly about gossip and the damage it causes. Yet despite this truth, gossip is often accepted in the workplace, neighborhoods, families, social gatherings, and among friends. Why is this?

A troublemaker plants seeds of strife; gossip separates the best of friends.

(Proverbs 16:28 NLT)

In Numbers 12:1–15 we read that Miriam and Aaron began talking against Moses because he had married a Cushite woman. But the Lord heard them and was very angry with them. Miriam's skin became as white as snow from leprosy. When Aaron saw what had happened to her, he begged Moses to go to God on her behalf. So Moses cried out to God to heal her. Even though Miriam was sent outside the camp for seven days, the Lord healed her.

Gossip attacks the young, old, male, female, married, unmarried, Christian, and non-Christian. Gossip is irretrievable: you can't take it back once it's out there. Gossip is unloving and offensive. It only tears people down. So why do we gossip? Perhaps because of a lack of healthy self-esteem, having nothing more important to say, boredom, habit, or the desire to fit into the crowd.

When we are being gossiped about, it's hard not to take offense because it hurts. But just as Moses petitioned God on Miriam's behalf, we are to pray with a heart of compassion, realizing that hurting people hurt others—and that God himself is our advocate.

When we gossip, just as Miriam was shut away for seven days, we may need to be shut away for a time with Jesus so that He can deal with our hearts. Words can build up or tear down, but again, they cannot be taken back once they have escaped our mouths. We must remember that anyone can find dirt. Be the one who finds the gold, who speaks life.

Let no corrupt word proceed out of your mouth,
but what is good for necessary edification,
that it may impart grace to the hearers.
(Ephesians 4:29 NKJV)

STUDY GUIDE
Daniel 6:22; Proverbs 18:21; Numbers 12:1–16;
James 3:7–16; Proverbs 11:27; Proverbs 31:26;
James 3:7–18; Numbers 12:1–15

PERSONAL REFLECTION
1. What is the motive behind your words?
2. Are you speaking life or death?

THE PRODIGAL

In Luke 15:11–32 we read a parable Jesus told about a wealthy man who had two sons. Both sons worked for their father, caring for his land and livestock. One day the younger son asked the father for his inheritance. According to Middle Eastern culture, it was a great offense for a child to ask for his inheritance before his father died. However, the father divided his wealth between his sons, and the youngest of the two packed his bags and left home. Traveling to a distant land, the young man, not mature enough to handle the treasure of wealth bestowed upon him, foolishly spent the money. Soon after his money was gone, a famine took place in the land. Destitute, the young man worked for a farmer feeding pigs. Eventually realizing that the pigs were better cared for than he was, the young man returned home to his father's house.

Upon the son's arrival, the father, filled with unconditional love and forgiveness, held no offense toward the younger son and welcomed him with open arms. However, the older son, who had faithfully worked on the father's farm, failed to grasp that everything his father owned was his. This misunderstanding led to resentment, a feeling that could have been avoided *if he had realized his true value* and security in his father's house.

Although many of us remain physically loyal by continuing to serve in the house of the Lord, some of us may harbor bitterness and resentment toward our brothers and sisters in Christ, believing that because their sins seem more evident, our siblings have no right to the treasures our heavenly Father has to give. Yet all the while, our hearts are corrupt and full of jealousy, thus failing to realize that all the redeemed are sons and daughters of God, and we continue living as orphans in our Father's house, unable to partake of the treasure set before us due to the condition of our hearts.

The prodigal, full of selfish desire, could be defined as someone who does not realize or appreciate the treasures of God, thus wasting it selfishly away. You may be able to relate to the prodigal son trying to find his way home. Or you may relate to the older brother, who stayed to help his father while harboring unforgiveness and anger, not realizing that all the Father has is ours. Either way, your heavenly Father has not given up on you. Instead, He is waiting with anticipation and open arms for your return home and for you to stop living as an orphan in the Father's house, knowing that all He has belongs to His children.

When assessing the wrongs of others, we must remember that God looks at the heart and not the outward appearance. Since humans cannot see what is in the hearts of others, we must look in a mirror before casting the first stone. Ask the Holy Spirit for a heart of compassion and love so that, just as the Father, we can welcome the prodigals home with open arms.

Let all bitterness, wrath, anger, clamor, and evil
speaking be put away from you, with all malice.
And be kind to one another, tenderhearted, forgiving
one another, even as God in Christ forgave you.
(Ephesians 4:31–32 NKJV)

STUDY GUIDE

Luke 15:11–32; Matthew 7:5; 1 John 1:8–9; John 8:7

PERSONAL REFLECTION

1. In what ways have you taken for granted the gifts God has given you?

2. Are you jealous and offended by the gifting and calling of others in the house of God?

HAIRBALLS IN THE SOUP

I don't know about you, but for me, sitting down at a restaurant in anticipation for a warm bowl of soup or a hot beverage on a cold winter day is a treasured moment that is both comforting and inviting. But finding someone's hair in my food or beverage makes my stomach turn, and I can no longer partake. A replacement bowl of soup or drink will not suffice because I no longer have an appetite for anything this establishment offers, and I will most likely never enter their door again.

I often compare this analogy with being hurt by those in the church who are supposed to love and care for us. Heartbreak of this kind has caused many to walk away from the church. Although some may immediately seek out another church to be a part of, others may take longer or decide never to return.

Those who choose to leave the church haven't necessarily turned their backs on God and their relationship with Him. God's healing is not confined to a physical location, but rather, it's about the state of your heart. There are times when it's necessary to remain where you are and confront the issues with those who have hurt you or those you may have hurt.

Sadly, I have to say there have been times when I have had to step out of the church environment to heal from the damage done to my heart. After all, it's hard to understand why the place we go to receive healing rubs salt in our wounds. Unfortunately, this salt does not bring healing but has lost its savor.

So why do we get hurt, and why do we hurt others within the church?

- It's a distraction for the devil to violate and separate the body of Christ. Thus, it causes us to change our focus from Christ to the offense.
- We do not know our true identity in Christ. Therefore, we tend to compete with one another as if one body part is greater than the other.
- We carry the offense in our hearts from previous experiences, thus allowing the baggage from our past to define our future. But it can limit our future only if we refuse to let it go.
- We are dislocated, not knowing where we belong in the body of Christ. We cannot function properly in the body if we do not understand our God-created purpose. Therefore, we must go to the giver of life and ask Him which part of the body He created us uniquely to function as.
- We choose to be offended rather than to walk in forgiveness and love, forgetting that holding offense in our hearts toward someone is our choice.
- The self in us dominates the Christ in us. Removing ourselves so Christ can shine through us is a process. It doesn't happen because we accepted Christ as our Savior. Removing self requires discipline in time spent with our Creator in prayer, worship, and study; it may sometimes require counseling to overcome things we have become accustomed to.

Forgiving can be challenging when instead, we want to give that person a piece of our mind. Our heavenly Father desires us to shower them with the love of Christ in us—because there isn't one thing that happens in life that the blood of Jesus has not covered.

Keep your heart with all diligence, for out
of it spring the issues of life.
(Proverbs 4:23 NKJV)

The cross we carry should make the statement of who Christ is and what He died for, not who and what *we* are. It should represent not the trials we're going through but rather the Christ in us.

Remember—there isn't anyone who deserves to be forgiven. Yet God in His infinite love gave His Son to forgive us. So when you're faced with the choice of holding onto anger or forgiving, ask yourself, *Can I find this unforgiving spirit in Jesus?* Since the answer is obviously no, then it's something you shouldn't want in you. Let the love and forgiveness of Christ guide your actions and decisions.

We will know we have truly forgiven when we can go to our heavenly Father and say, "Don't hold that person accountable for what he [she] has done to me. Instead, forgive him [her], Father, because this person really does not know what he [she] is doing."

Don't let the hairballs in the soup cause you to stop eating it. Instead, ask your heavenly Father where the body of Christ is that you are to be a part of so you can function fully in your God-given ability. Then ask Him to show you how to check your baggage at heaven's gate—because forgiving others will set you free!

We do not wrestle against flesh and blood, but against principalities, against powers, against the rulers of the darkness of this age, against spiritual hosts of wickedness in the heavenly places.

(Ephesians 6:12 NKJV)

STUDY GUIDE
Romans 12:4–5; Matthew 18:15–20; Proverbs 21:31;
John 4:20; Galatians 5:13–15; 1 Corinthians 12:18–31;
Ephesians 4:31–32; 2 Corinthians 3:18; Matthew 16:24;
John 12:24–26; Luke 9:24–25; Acts 7:59–60

PERSONAL REFLECTION
1. Have you been hurt by those who were supposed to love and help you heal? Or have you been the offender?
2. Ask the Holy Spirit to heal your heart as you give all those hurts to Him. Describe your journey of healing.

HE WOULD HAVE PASSED BY

We read in Mark 6:45–51 that immediately after feeding the five thousand men and their families, Jesus sent the multitude home. After they were all gone, Jesus went to the mountain alone to pray. When evening came, the boat the disciples were in was in the middle of the sea, and Jesus, alone on the land, saw that they were struggling at rowing against the wind and came toward them, walking on water about the fourth watch of the night. Jesus intended to pass them by, but they cried out, thinking He was a ghost. "Don't be afraid," He told them. "It's me." Then, as He climbed into the boat, the wind stopped. The disciples were amazed. They didn't understand the miracle Jesus had done earlier that day of feeding the people with five loaves of bread and two fish because their hearts had become hardened.

Jesus would have passed by them, except they cried out. I've thought of this verse often throughout the years. How often have we failed to recognize His presence or call out His name? How many times have our hearts become so calloused that we think nothing of His mercy and grace toward us and the miracles He has done in our lives?

One reason Jesus would have passed by is that He doesn't abide in fear. He wanted the disciples to call out to Him. When they cried out, they welcomed His presence of peace amid the storm. Notice that the wind stopped as soon as Jesus climbed into the boat. When Jesus walked on the water, the disciples did not recognize Him, but Jesus recognized them.

Alternatively, the disciples might have blamed God for the storm. It's a common reaction to blame God when life's storms hit and things don't go our way. We might find ourselves blaming Him for the uncomfortable paths we tread, unaware that it's precisely in these storms that Christ can shape and strengthen our character, offering us a chance for transformation and growth.

If we recognize His presence and praise Him amidst the storm, knowing He will never leave or forsake us instead of allowing our hearts to become hardened by offense and fear, He will bless us in a way we could never imagine as His character is developed in us along the way.

STUDY GUIDE
Mark 6:45–51; Hebrews 3:7–8

PERSONAL REFLECTION

1. Is your heart filled with fear, causing you to not recognize Jesus when He passes by?
2. Or—are you calling out His name in praise amidst the storm? Journal your thoughts.

STEPS TOWARD FORGIVENESS

In most cases the offense is only a distraction to keep us bound, to keep us from serving the Lord with our whole hearts. Forgiveness can be challenging, and in many situations it takes time. It's important to remember that forgiveness isn't about pretending or about forgetting that we were ever hurt. It's about acknowledging that hurt and then releasing others so we can be set free. The Greek word translated as *forgiveness* literally means "letting go."

For many, amidst the pain and sorrow, we take offense and harbor unforgiveness toward those living in fear and who are resentful themselves. Thus, the misdirected hurt runs rampant toward anyone in the way.

"Whatever you want men to do to you, do also to them."
(Matthew 7:12 NKJV)

Forgiving those who have wronged us is a condition of our hearts. It does not mean we must welcome that person back into our lives. Nor does it mean we always have to go to the person and tell the person that we forgive him or her—because in some situations this may be impossible. Each case is unique and should be dealt with uniquely with the Holy Spirit as our guide. Directing our focus from offense to forgiveness isn't easy, but with God's help we can do it.

Here are some steps that you can take toward a life of forgiveness:

- Refocus. Change your focus from the situation to Jesus.
  Set your mind on things above, not on things on the earth.
  (Colossians 3:2 NKJV)
- Pray for your offender.
  "Love your enemies, bless those who curse you, do good to those who hate you, and pray for those who spitefully use you and persecute you" (Matthew 5:44 NKJV).
- Reevaluate your heart posture so you can see clearly.
  Keep your heart with all diligence, for out of it spring the issues of life (Proverbs 4:23 NKJV).
- Ask God for direction.
  Wisdom is the principal thing; therefore get wisdom. And in all your getting, get understanding (Proverbs 4:7 NKJV).
- Ask God to give you a heart of praise.
  I will bless the Lord at all times; His praise shall continually be in my mouth (Psalm 34:1 NKJV).
- Ask God to develop His character within you.
  If any of you lacks wisdom, let him ask of God, who gives to all liberally and without reproach, and it will be given to him (James 1:5 NKJV).
- Above all, let love be your guide.
  Be imitators of God as dear children. And walk in love, as Christ also has loved us and given Himself for us, an offering and a sacrifice to God for a sweet-smelling aroma (Ephesians 5:1–2 NKJV).

Sin shall not have dominion over you,
for you are not under law but under grace.
(Romans 6:14 NKJV)

STUDY GUIDE

Hebrews 12:1; Romans 12:2; Romans 12:9–21

PERSONAL REFLECTION

1. Is there someone you need to forgive? Journal your thoughts.
2. Are you willing to acknowledge the pain and trust God to heal your heart?

LIFE APPLICATION

Heavenly Father,

I ask you to soften my heart, which has become calloused by the cares of this world. Please help me to forgive others, as you have forgiven me. Some of the wounds are so deep that they have become infected, and you are the only one who can heal them. So as I give them to you, I ask that you set free those I have held captive and help me to love them with a love that only you can provide. Father, forgive me for harboring unforgiveness toward others. And as I cast all my cares on you, please heal my heart. Thank you for being my healer and for your forgiveness. From now on, please help me choose forgiveness over offense—and to look for the gold in others.

In your name I pray.

Amen

5
MINDSET

What You Believe Will Either Hold
You Captive or Set You Free

MINDSET: INTRODUCTION

Life's most significant obstacle for me has been overcoming the battlefield of my mind. As humans, we find that it's easier to believe lies than the truth of God's Word. When mined properly, our thoughts can be as uncut gems leading along the pathway to a godly character. But once polished and shaped by the Word of God and a right relationship with the Savior, our mindset can lead us to the treasure chest of the kingdom of heaven, which is the character of Christ. It's not our circumstances but our attitude that changes our character to become more Christ-like.

Many times that begins with the way we think. Jesus taught only kingdom principles during His three short years of ministry on the earth. He spoke, demonstrated, and lived it. Because Jesus *is* the kingdom of heaven, His character results from that.

I have found that life takes on a new meaning when I position my heart in heaven, where Jesus resides at the Father's right hand—because my life is all about glorifying God on the earth through whatever is happening around or in me. It was never supposed to be about me. Life has not been easy, but I have learned not to conform to the things of this world but to be transformed by the renewing of my mind through the Word of God. I have learned a kingdom mindset and how to function in it. Although I have a long way to go, the journey thus far has been incredible.

Verbal, emotional, mental, and spiritual abuse can be as bad as or worse than physical abuse. In my experience, there was a honeymoon period between one bout of physical abuse and the next—a reprieve. But the emotional, verbal, and mental abuse never stopped.

Even at times in a spiritual setting, when I thought I was safe after I got out of the situation, as hard and as scary as it was, the words continued playing over and over in my head: that I was not good enough and I never would be. I felt as if I couldn't do anything right. And the lies I had been told for so many years had become my truth.

Breaking free from believing the lies is difficult because the programming has gone on for years. I didn't know who I was or who I was supposed to be—until the Holy Spirit stepped in and gave me such a hunger for the Word of God that I couldn't help but treasure every word as it became alive in me. As I received the truth of His Word, my shattered heart began to heal, and I drew closer to Him in the process.

As we step into this chapter, I invite you to embark on a deeply personal journey, exploring the keys I've discovered to unlock the treasure of the kingdom of heaven. As we dig into the experiences of our forefathers, you'll find yourself on a transformational path. You will discover how the Spirit of Christ residing within you can revolutionize your life, enabling you to perceive and live from a heavenly perspective on earth. You will develop a more intimate relationship with Christ by spending time with Him in worship, prayer, and biblical study as you embrace childlike faith and develop a heart like His.

"The kingdom of God does not come with observation. . . .
For indeed, the kingdom of God is within you."

(Luke 17:20–21 NKJV)

BREAKING FREE

Our past can define us or catapult us into our future. It all depends on our mindset. We can never go forward if we always look in the rearview mirror. None of us are immune to the trials of life. But when we refuse to let go of the past, we remain a victim of it by remaining in the same mindset that has held us captive.

In Acts 16:16–40 we read that Paul and Silas were beaten, bound in chains, and thrown into prison for preaching the gospel. However, instead of falling victim to their circumstances, they prayed and sang worship songs to the Lord. As the sound of praise filled the prison, the chains holding them and the other prisoners fell off. Because Paul and Silas were filled with the Spirit of the Lord before they were imprisoned, looking beyond their current circumstances was not an issue. Instead of focusing on what had been done to them, they focused on the Christ in them.

Changing our mindset is a journey and at times a downright struggle. Perhaps heartache and hardships are all you have known. Or perhaps you have come from a good background but life circumstances have not been in your favor. You may have made wrong choices and the consequences of those choices have been hard to bear and seem never-ending.

It is as if your eyesight has become dim because you have lived in the darkness of destructive thinking for far too long. But if you keep pursuing God, you will become accustomed to the light of His Word, thus allowing you to break free from the chains that seem to bind you and enter a new life in Him.

No temptation has overtaken you except such as is common to man; but God is faithful, who will not allow you to be tempted beyond what you are able, but with the temptation will also make the way of escape, that you may be able to bear it.

(1 Corinthians 10:13 NKJV)

STUDY GUIDE
Acts 16:16–40; Matthew 16:19

PERSONAL REFLECTION

1. Are you able to praise God whatever your circumstance?
2. Does your attitude change the atmosphere of your environment?

CHANGE OF HEART

We see no need for change when everything seems to be going well. But even if our lives change for the better and we have no desire to return to the way things were, we may find ourselves revisiting the familiar place for lack of a better plan. I can relate to this through my journey. For instance, after I experienced a spiritual awakening, I occasionally slipped back into old habits, like Peter and some other disciples who returned to their lives as fishermen after Jesus went to the cross.

In Luke 5:5–8 we read that the disciples had been fishing all night but had caught nothing. At dawn, Jesus was standing on the shore, and He called out, asking them if they had caught any fish. They answered no. Then He told them to throw out their nets on the other side of the boat. They did as Jesus said and caught so many fish that they couldn't haul in the net. When they arrived at the shore, Jesus served them a breakfast of fish and bread that He had prepared for them. This is the third time Jesus had appeared to His disciples since He had risen from the dead. After breakfast, Jesus asked Peter three times if he loved Him. Each time Peter answered, "Yes, Lord. You know I love you," to which Jesus replied, "Feed my sheep."

I believe Jesus wanted Peter to position his heart where Jesus was. Because when you know Jesus and have spent time with Him, you cannot go back to your old way of life. And if you follow His direction and listen to His words, which are written in the Bible, you will find He has a bigger plan for your life.

"Do not remember the former things, nor consider the things of old. Behold, I will do a new thing, now it shall spring forth; shall you not know it? I will even make a road in the wilderness and rivers in the desert."

(Isaiah 43:18–19 NKJV)

STUDY GUIDE

Matthew 4:18–20; John 21:1–6; Ephesians 4:22–24

PERSONAL REFLECTION

1. After coming to know Jesus, what part of your former life that does not glorify God have you found hard to give up?
2. Why?

LOOSED AND UNBOUND

Artists often visualize the finished project before they begin, and when they stick to what their minds see, minor distractions cannot stand in the way of their finished work of art. God, the master craftsman, saw you before you were formed in your mother's womb. His purpose was not to create a life without setbacks but to use these challenges to help develop and shape our character. He has always seen you from the kingdom perspective of His original finished masterpiece, a perspective filled with profound love and unwavering care for you.

In John 11:1–44 we read that when Jesus was in Jerusalem, He received word from Mary and Martha asking Him to come to Bethany because their brother, Lazarus, was sick and dying. Even though Jesus loved Mary, Martha, and Lazarus, he remained where He was for two more days before leaving for Bethany. When he arrived in Bethany, only two miles from Jerusalem, Jesus found that Lazarus had been in the tomb for four days. Despite Lazarus' being dead and buried, Jesus saw the situation from a divine perspective. He saw Lazarus through God the Father's eyes rather than man's. Jesus understood that this seemingly insurmountable setback for Lazarus in man's eyes was all a part of God's plan. It was the start of a new beginning for Lazarus and those around the tomb that day, because God saw the end before the beginning and had provided a way out of the tomb for Lazarus before Lazarus was ever in the grave.

Jesus went to the tomb where Lazarus was and told him to come out. He did not tell Lazarus to rise up or come to life, nor did He breathe into Lazarus. He simply shouted, "Come out!" As Lazarus walked slowly out of the tomb, Jesus told those standing nearby to unbind him.

Amidst the gloom that may surround us, we are not confined to that place. From the beginning of time, God has crafted a unique plan for your life. Allow Him to set you free from the constraints of your earthly thinking. This will enable you to perceive life from a kingdom perspective, a perspective that holds the promise of profound transformation, knowing that God envisioned you, His masterpiece, long before your existence. You must remember that a few bumps along the way have not altered His divine plan for your life.

Sometimes things happen for the glory of God. So come out from the old mindset you have become accustomed to, take off the grave clothes of your earthly thinking, and begin viewing yourself from heaven's perspective. Because God has always had a plan for your life. And His kingdom can come on earth just as it is in heaven, beginning with how you think.

When we begin seeing things through the eyes of His Spirit within us, it will change how we think and develop a kingdom mindset within us.

As we learn to perceive the world through the lens of His Spirit within us, our thoughts undergo a profound transformation. This shift in perspective fosters the development of a "kingdom mindset," a way of thinking that aligns with God's perspective and purposes within us, leading not just to spiritual growth but also to a deeper sense of personal fulfillment and enlightenment.

You are a slave to whatever controls you.

(2 Peter 2:19 NLT)

STUDY GUIDE

John 11:1–44; Romans 8:37–39

PERSONAL REFLECTION

1. What part of your thought life is still bound up in the things of the past?
2. Are you ready to walk unbound out of the past into your future?

WHO'S TO BLAME?

How often do we miss the blessings God has prepared for us because of our limited thinking? Instead of taking responsibility for our lives, we often find ourselves blaming others for our lack of progress. But imagine the potential for personal growth if we were to shift our focus inward, engaging in self-reflection and taking ownership of our actions.

We read in John 5:1–15 that Jesus went to Jerusalem for a Jewish holy day. Inside the city was a pool that had five covered porches. At a specific time of year, an angel entered the pool and stirred up the water. After the angel had stirred the water, whoever stepped into the pool first was healed of whatever disease he or she had. Crowds of sick people would lie on the porches waiting for the moving of the water. One of the men lying there had been sick for thirty-eight years. Jesus saw him and, knowing he had been ill for a long time, asked him, "Do you want to get well?" The sick man, not realizing whom He was talking to, replied, "I can't be healed because I have no one to put me into the water when it is stirred. While trying to get into the water, someone else always enters before me." Jesus told the man to stand up, take his mat, and walk. Instantly the man was healed. Later Jesus saw him in the temple and said to him, "Now that you are well, stop sinning."

How is it possible for a man to sin, who could do nothing but lie by a pool for thirty-eight years? We know that he chose to blame others for why he had not been healed. And if all he could do was lie there, then the sin within his life was in his heart, mind, and mouth. He needed a change of heart! This story serves as a powerful reminder of the importance of personal accountability and the need for a change in mindset.

"A good man out of the good treasure of his heart brings forth good; and an evil man out of the evil treasure of his heart brings forth evil. For out of the abundance of his heart his mouth speaks."

(Luke 6:45 NKJV)

How many of life's situations could be different if we chose to think differently and obey God, praising Him in the good and the bad? Instead, we wait for someone else to put us into the water while complaining about our situation. What if we put on our running shoes and got in the race rather than waiting for someone else to drag us behind him or her or push us forward?

Do we hinder our own prosperity by not fully obeying God's Word and the instructions He gives us? When we stand before Him in heaven, we will be held accountable for our choices. When God asks, "What did you do with the talent [life] I gave you?" what will your answer be? Our actions are our own, and blame-placing has no place in the kingdom of God.

Fix your thoughts on what is true, and honorable, and right, and pure, and lovely, and admirable. Think about things that are excellent and worthy of praise.

(Philippians 4:8 NLT)

STUDY GUIDE

John 5:1–15; Philippians 2:14; Romans 12:2; Romans 14:12;
Psalm 34:1–2; 2 Chronicles 24:20; Galatians 6:5;
Matthew 25:14–30

PERSONAL REFLECTION

1. What would life be like if we changed our way of thinking and speaking?
2. Whom have you been blaming for where you are in your life?

WHEN VIPERS BITE

One of the most debilitating forces in life is the lies we believe about ourselves. We base our feelings on our imaginations. What we think about ourselves will show up in how we treat others, which in most cases stems from a false belief that we have accepted as truth.

On the contrary, those who truly know the love of the Father will love as He loves and will bring healing to those they come in contact with. But the question is "How do we get there?"

We read in Acts 28:3–5 that after being shipwrecked by a storm, Paul gathered an armful of sticks and laid them on a fire. A poisonous snake driven out by the heat bit him on the hand. Seeing this, the people waited for him to die. But Paul shook the snake off into the fire and was unharmed.

It's not whether or not the vipers bite but if you allow the venom to kill you. We cannot control how other people treat us, but we can control how we respond to their behavior. We can walk around with arrows in our backs or know that God's got our back. So stop allowing the world to invade your heart by how you think—and renew your mind with the Word of God because the venom can destroy you only if you let it.

Warren Buffet said, "You will continue to suffer if you react emotionally to everything said to you. True power is sitting back and observing things with logic. True power is restraint. If words control you, that means everyone else can control you. So breathe and allow things to pass."

Our worth is not measured by what others think, feel, or say about us. God's opinion of us measures our value.

"You will keep him in perfect peace, whose mind is stayed on You, because he trusts in You."

(Isaiah 26:3 NKJV)

STUDY GUIDE

Psalm 119:29; Philippians 4:8–9; Acts 28:3–5; Matthew 16:18;
Romans 12:2; 1 Peter 4:8; Proverbs 29:25–27

PERSONAL REFLECTION

1. How do you react when negative words are spoken to you or about you?
2. In what ways can you change your behavior by the way you think?

MATTERS OF THE HEART

We read in Genesis 29—35 about a woman named Rachel, who left her homeland with her husband, Jacob, whom she shared with her sister, Leah. She stole her father's idols, and when he came looking for them, she was sitting on the bag they were in and told Laban, her father, that she could not get up because she was menstruating.

Rachel came from a lying trickster family. Her aunt Rebekah (Jacob's mother) encouraged and helped her son Jacob lie to his dying father, Isaac, so that Jacob would receive the firstborn blessing instead of Esau. Rachel's father, Laban, was a liar, a thief, and a trickster. And Rachel, rather than choosing to change the way she thought, adapted to the practices of her family heritage. She decided to embrace the same mindset she had been raised in and remain in that familiar place.

God blessed Rachel with a husband who loved her dearly, two sons to whom she gave birth, and two sons by her handmaiden. But Rachel was never happy, just like her father, Laban. She continued wanting more. Why Rachel stole her father's idols is unclear. Perhaps it was because that even though she believed in Jacob's God, she never fully embraced Him as the one true God. Maybe she felt that since she wasn't getting everything she wanted from Jacob's God, she would pray to the idols of her father, Laban.

God had a plan for Rachel's life, and He fulfilled His plan by allowing her to be one of the mothers' wombs from which the twelve tribes of Israel came. But shortly after giving birth to her second son, Benjamin, Rachel died at a young age. As a result, she could never enjoy her children or grandchildren.

Her youngest son never even had the opportunity to know his mother. All those years of constant competing, complaining, and being unhappy robbed her of enjoying God's blessings. Rather than trusting His plan for her life and being grateful, Rachel felt her plan was better. Joseph, Rachel's firstborn from her womb, became a powerful, mighty man, just as God had destined him to be. But Rachel could never rejoice with him in fulfilling his destiny because of her selfish heart.

In the book of Ruth (1–4) we read about a woman named Ruth, who was a Moabite, born and raised in a pagan belief system in which people worshiped many idol gods and sacrificed their children. As a Moabite going to Naomi's homeland of Judah, the Judean people would most likely reject Ruth. Yet Ruth decided to leave everything she had ever known because of her love for Naomi and Naomi's God. Ruth could have become bitter and angry because she had lost her husband and had no children. But she chose to be loving and kind. However, Naomi was upset because of the loss of her husband and sons. She even told her friends in Judah to call her "Mara," which means "bitter," because she felt God had dealt bitterly with her. I'm sure that Naomi, being bitter, wasn't easy to live with. Although Naomi encouraged Ruth to stay in Moab, Ruth chose to remain faithful to Naomi and to the one true God she had come to know.

In Judah, God blessed Ruth abundantly, and she was able to gather grain from a field she didn't own and hadn't planted. She later married the field owner from whom she had collected the grain and gave birth to a son named Obed, who became the father of Jesse, the father of David, and all were in the lineage of Jesus. There are only two books in the Bible named after women, and Ruth is one of them because of her heart to serve her love and devotion and her choice to walk away from the familiar place into the unknown, trusting God for the outcome.

> *"I, the Lord, search the heart, I test the mind,*
> *even to give every man according to his ways,*
> *according to the fruit of his doings."*
> (Jeremiah 17:10 NKJV)

STUDY GUIDE

Genesis 29–35; Ruth 1–4; Mark 12:30–31

PERSONAL REFLECTION

1. Where have the desires of your heart led you astray?
2. Does deception or integrity rule your heart? In what way?

POISON ACID

In Acts 3:1–11 we read about a lame man sitting at the temple entrance, often begging for money from those going to worship. When he saw Peter and John going into the temple, he begged them for money, thinking it would help meet his needs. Peter told the man, "I don't have any money, but I will give you what I have." Then *Peter told the man to pay attention,* and as he reached out and took the man by the hand, Peter helped the man to his feet and told him to stand up and walk in the name of Jesus Christ. At that moment the man began walking, leaping, and praising God.

Notice that the man had legs but couldn't walk on them. Therefore, he became accustomed to the only way of life he had ever known, perhaps not realizing there may be another solution to his problem rather than the Band-aid fix of sitting at the temple entrance begging for money.

There are those in the body of Christ who have become victims of the circumstances surrounding them. They choose to remain in the victim mindset because of their past, expecting to be spoon-fed God's Word. Although they desire to be healed, their hearts cannot receive it because of the thought process they choose to remain in. It is as if they had swallowed a poisonous acid that has left them with holes in their heart. Fear, unforgiveness, bitterness, jealousy, greed, slander, lust, and the desire for things of the world have eaten away at the core of their being. And rather than seek healthy solutions for themselves, they blame others for where they are in life and expect others to fix their problem.

Have you ever heard "You are what you eat"? Just as a balanced diet and healthy lifestyle promote physical well-being, an unhealthy diet can lead to illness. The same principle applies to our minds. What we consume mentally influences our spiritual health. Therefore, we must always be cautious of what our minds digest. Unfortunately, many individuals remain in the same lifestyle of what has held them captive as they continue feeding on the rotten source of their problems.

Some people go through life thinking they know what they need, all the while asking others to fix their problems with nothing more than what seems to be Band-aid solutions—therefore providing temporary fixes with no permanent solution to the problems, as Band-aids continue to be applied to the continued bleeding.

We will always need others to spoon-feed us if we continue allowing the acid within our hearts to eat away at us by refusing to change our thoughts. Our friends, family, church, pastor, job, or finances will never be able to fulfill the empty places in our hearts. Only Jesus can take away our sorrows, and only He can satisfy our hearts' longing.

As Peter instructed the lame man to pay attention, we too must be mindful of what we feed our souls and spirits. Often our focus becomes so fixated on the problem that we overlook the solution. We neglect wise counsel and guidance, opting for temporary fixes that may intensify the issues. It begins with our thoughts. We must ask God to illuminate our hearts, to help us see clearly and step out of the fog of our problems into the clear vision of His love and grace.

*It is impossible to please God without faith. Anyone
who wants to come to him must believe that God exists
and that he rewards those who sincerely seek him.*

(Hebrews 11:6 NLT)

STUDY GUIDE

Acts 3:1–11; 2 Chronicles 7:14–15; Jeremiah 29:11–13;
Isaiah 59:1; Matthew 11:28–30

PERSONAL REFLECTION

1. Have you continued filling yourself with the things of this world while expecting others to fill you with the Word of God?

2. What might happen if you start pursuing God and a relationship with Him?

A TREE WITH A VIEW

In Luke 19:1–10 we read about Zacchaeus, a little man in a prominent position, a chief tax collector who had become very rich. One day Jesus passed through Jericho, and Zacchaeus wanted to see who Jesus was. Unable to see over the large crowd because he was too short, Zacchaeus ran ahead and climbed a sycamore tree.

When Jesus passed by, He looked up in the tree and called Zacchaeus by name, inviting Himself to be a guest in Zacchaeus' home. Overwhelmed with joy, Zacchaeus came down from the tree and welcomed Jesus into his home. The crowd grumbled and complained that Jesus would choose to go to the home of a man known for his sins. Yet acknowledging his past wrongdoings, Zacchaeus stood before the Lord and declared, "I will give half my possessions to the poor, and if I have cheated anyone, I will pay back four times the amount." In response, Jesus proclaimed, "Today salvation has come to your house."

Though small in stature, Zacchaeus would stop at nothing to attain the desires of his heart. And that day his desire to see Jesus was more significant than the crowd who had gathered or his pride. So with childlike faith, Zacchaeus ran ahead of the crowd of people and climbed a tree. Notice that he had to climb a little higher from where he was, with childlike faith, full of wonder and humility. Zacchaeus didn't care that he had gained much of the world's riches—he just wanted to see Jesus.

Although Zacchaeus never called out to Jesus so anyone could hear him from the tree, Jesus stopped and called Zacchaeus by name because He recognized a heart of repentance hidden from others, sitting in a tree with a view. Zacchaeus discovered a key to the kingdom of heaven that day by positioning his heart in childlike faith to see Jesus. As a result, he was recognized by the Son of God and called by name.

Nothing in all creation is hidden from God. Everything is naked and exposed before his eyes, and he is the one to whom we are accountable.

(Hebrews 4:13 NLT)

STUDY GUIDE
Luke 19:1–10; Matthew 18:1–6

PERSONAL REFLECTION

1. Do you believe God can change your life?
2. Are you willing to humble yourself in the place where Jesus is?

THE LIES WE BELIEVE

*"I will be your Father, and you will be my sons
and daughters, says the Lord Almighty."*
(2 Corinthians 6:18 NLT)

The fall of man did not begin with a hunger for a piece of forbidden fruit but rather with believing a lie, which led to Adam and Eve questioning their identity as children of God. Eating from the tree was an act of disobedience after the lie was told and believed, followed by shame, blame-placing, jealousy, murder, and so on. If Adam and Eve had known their identity, they would have never accepted the lie.

In Matthew 3:13–17 we read that the heavens opened as Jesus came out of the water after being baptized by John the Baptist, and the Spirit of God descended like a dove and settled on Jesus. A voice was heard from heaven saying, "This is my beloved Son. In Him I am well pleased." Jesus' identity had already been established in heaven by the Father, but this was a revelation to those on earth.

Immediately after His baptism, Jesus was led into the wilderness to fast and pray for forty days. Despite the Spirit of God proclaiming Jesus' identity as the Son of God just forty days earlier, the devil attempted to sow seeds of doubt in Jesus' mind about His true identity.

When you received Christ as your Savior, you were adopted into the family of God. Nothing or no one can take that away from you. You are His! The devil's greatest fear is that you know your God-given identity, because when you see the truth, it sets you free from the lies you once believed.

The only one keeping you from your destiny is you. The voices we hear most loudly are the ones in our own heads. So stop believing the lies in your mind about what the world says about you—and start thinking about what God says about you. Because if God is for you, no one can be against you. And you can do all things through Christ, who is your strength. Think about what is honorable, pure, loving, and kind, things that are excellent and worthy of praise.

Just as the first step to humanity's fall was believing a lie, the first step to freedom is accepting the truth and allowing it to set you free. You will then begin to discover who God created you to be.

STUDY GUIDE

Genesis 3:1–14; Matthew 3:13–17; Matthew 4:1–11;
Romans 8:31; Philippians 4:13; Philippians 4:8;
Zephaniah 3:17

PERSONAL REFLECTION

1. What are some lies you have come to believe?
2. Are you willing to discover the truth of what God's Word says about you?

STUCK IN LO-DEBAR

Many have gone through life feeling rejected or not good enough. Fear, anxiety, and depression run rampant, taking over our thoughts about life and ourselves. Honesty and kindness seem to be a thing of the past, especially to oneself. Many would choose to believe the lie about themselves and what the world has led them to believe rather than the truth of who God created them to be and who He says they are.

In 2 Samuel 9:1–13 we read about King David, who summoned a man named Ziba, a former servant of King Saul, and asked him, "Is anyone from Saul's family still alive? If so, I want to show God's kindness to them as I promised Jonathan I would."

Ziba told David, "One of Jonathan's sons is still alive. And His name is Mephibosheth. He is unable to walk, and he lives in Lo-debar."

So David sent for Mephibosheth. When Mephibosheth came to David, he bowed low to the ground in deep respect and fear. "Don't be afraid," David told him. "I intend to show kindness to you, to honor the promise I made to your father, Jonathan. I will give you all of the property that once belonged to your grandfather, King Saul, and you will eat here with me at the king's table."

Mephibosheth bowed respectfully and asked, "Who am I, that you would show such kindness to a dead dog like me?"

Then King David summoned King Saul's former servant Ziba and said, "I have given Mephibosheth, your master's grandson, everything that belonged to King Saul and his family. You and your sons and servants are to farm the land for him to produce food for his household. But Mephibosheth, King Saul's grandson, will eat here at my table like one of my sons."

The meaning of *Mephibosheth* is "the mouth of shame." Lo-debar is a place of no pasture, where one has been in the wilderness, isolated and lonely. In biblical times Lo-debar was also considered a ghetto town.

When Mephibosheth came to David, he expected to be killed and fell to his face. Even though Mephibosheth was the grandson of a king and had royal blood running through his veins, he continued speaking from a mouth of shame concerning himself. We see this example when he asks David, "Who am I, that you would show such kindness to a dead dog like me?" With no hope, Mephibosheth lived in Lo-debar, a place of wilderness, isolation, desolation, and lack. He feared being killed by King David, who had taken his grandfather's position on the throne. But even though Mephibosheth could not walk and Lo-debar was where he planned to live and die, God had a better plan for Mephibosheth. Because God's intent was for Mephibosheth to live as the royalty that he was. So God spoke to King David's heart about Mephibosheth's royal heritage and provided a way out of Lo-debar, the place of wilderness, isolation, desolation, and lack. And from that day on, Mephibosheth ate at King David's table just as one of his sons.

Many of us have been trapped in the mindset of Lo-debar for far too long. We've allowed shame and fear of rejection to define us, living under a false identity that is not our own. But Christ the King has a different vision for us. He wants to restore us to our original, God-given identity, where we are seen as His beloved sons and daughters. He invites us to His table, not as outcasts but as cherished members of His family. Will you accept His invitation and step out of the mindset of Lo-debar?

> *As many as received Him, to them He gave*
> *them the right to become children of God,*
> *to those who believe in His name.*
>
> (John 1:12 NKJV)

STUDY GUIDE

2 Samuel 9:1–13; Ephesians 1:1–6

PERSONAL REFLECTION

1. Have you been living in the mindset of Lo-debar under the false identity of fear, rejection, and shame?
2. Have you felt unworthy to accept the King of heaven's invitation to sit at His table?

LIFE APPLICATION

Thank you, Father, that you have given me a spirit not of fear—but of power, love, and a sound mind. Open my eyes that I will see, my ears that I will hear, and soften my heart, making it pliable in your hands. Develop within me a greater desire to spend time with you. Help me change the way I think so that I can fully receive your love for me and fulfill your calling on my life. Forgive me for the selfishness and pride that I have allowed to hold me captive, thus forsaking the truth of your Word and believing the lies. Help me reflect your love to others from this moment on as I dedicate my thought life completely to you. Thank you, Father, for giving me the privilege of serving you. Thank you for your mercy and your grace.

Amen

6
PROVISION

It's Always Been There

PROVISION: INTRODUCTION

Throughout history the treasure of God's provision has always been there for us. He cares about every aspect of our lives and is not restricted to only one way of providing for our needs. However, His gems of provision may often be disguised as stepping stones that we fail to recognize, because His provision doesn't always come in the way we expect. But He always provides, and I am a testament to that, as well as those we are told of in Scripture, who have gone on before.

Throughout my years I have witnessed God's provision in the lives of others and myself multiple times—from the single mom without any earthly provision and all the bills due to the provision of the healing hand of God in circumstances where it seemed all hope was gone.

The first time I experienced the provision of God in my life was as a second-grader. Our class assignment was to create a booklet about a president of the United States. I was assigned

George Washington and worked very hard on my assignment. When I had finished, I put it in the basket on the teacher's desk. But somehow, the next day my booklet had disappeared. The teacher accused me of lying to her and not doing the assignment. She was angry with me and did not allow me to go to recess or participate in fun classroom activities. This continued for about a week, and I would go home upset from school each day. My mom and I would kneel next to the bed at night and pray, asking God for my George Washington booklet to be found.

One day when I went to school, my booklet was sitting right in front of the teacher on her desk. I remember it as if it were yesterday. God saw the cry of a little girl's heart and answered her prayer to provide a way out of lies that someone else believed about her. The teacher knew I could not have produced the quality of booklet I did in the short time since it had been missing. And she had no explanation of where the booklet had been or how it had suddenly appeared on her desk. But wherever it was, I believe it was placed in front of her on her desk by the hand of God—because He cared about the desire and need of a little girl's heart who came to Him in prayer.

As you read this chapter, I pray memories of God's provision for you will flood your mind, strengthening your faith in Him. I also pray that you will be able to step out in confidence, knowing that your heavenly Father has already been wherever you are going and has prepared the way.

THE FULL ARMOR OF GOD

We read in 1 Samuel 17:38–51 that when David as a boy went out to fight Goliath, Saul gave David his armor to wear. Although David tried on Saul's armor, it didn't fit, so he refused to wear it. There are several reasons that Saul's armor did not fit David. One of the most significant is that David was already wearing the armor of God. Another armor would have been much too confining!

Scripture tells us to put on the whole armor of God so that we can stand firm against all strategies of evil because we wrestle not against flesh and blood but against the unseen powers and principalities of darkness in this world. Therefore, we are to put on all of God's armor so that after the battle we will still be standing firm.

But what is the whole armor of God? *Ephesians 6:10–18*

- **The belt of truth:** Jesus said, "I am the way, the truth, and the life."
- **The breastplate of righteousness:** God is righteous in everything He does.
- **The shoes of peace:** God promises perfect peace to all who trust in Him.
- **The shield of faith:** Faith comes by hearing the Word of God.
- **The helmet of salvation:** God gave His only Son so that all who believe in Him would have eternal life.
- **The sword of the Spirit:** God's Word is powerful and sharper than the sharpest two-edged sword.

God desires for us to develop a Christ-like character by spending time with Him. He provides the whole armor of God, not only for David to wear but for us as well. Our heavenly Father invites us to draw closer to Him because it is in Him that our provision lies. As the essence of God's armor is revealed in us, a portrait of Christ is relevant to all we encounter.

We are not to be entangled with fear. We must know whose provision we operate in and that God always provides what we need when needed. Therefore, we can be at peace on the journey because He has already prepared the way ahead of us. So we can praise Him in the journey, for His protection is already upon us.

God uniquely designed us with a fingerprint all our own, and our armors are designed to fit us perfectly, just as David's did for the task set before him. Therefore, we cannot try wearing another person's armor to fight our battles because we must be able to move about freely without confinement as God develops His character within us so that we can walk into our destiny.

The Lord is righteous in all His ways,
gracious in all His works.
(Psalm 145:17 NKJV)

STUDY GUIDE

1 Samuel 17:38–51; Ephesians 6:10–18; John 14:6;
Psalm 11:7; Isaiah 26:3; Romans 10:17; John 3:16;
Hebrews 4:12; Psalm 145:14–16

PERSONAL REFLECTION

1. Are you wearing the whole armor of God?
2. If not, which part are you missing?

FIVE SMOOTH STONES

Life situations can sometimes lead us on a pathway of stepping stones. But what if each stepping stone led you on a journey of discovery to the destiny God has prepared for you and was packed with jewels along the way just for you? Many of us will stop and adorn ourselves with the gems and remain there because we see no need to continue the journey. Beyond the former stepping stones is a beautiful pathway leading to a larger treasure chest full of more valuable jewels than the first. Many never receive the fullness of all God has for them because they settle for what is at the beginning of the pathway instead of continuing on the journey, thinking that is all there is and wondering why God didn't answer their prayers or provide for their needs.

My God shall supply all your need according to His riches in glory by Christ Jesus.
(Philippians 4:19 NKJV)

We often stop short along the way, denying ourselves the full blessing ahead, where a more significant blessing awaits.

In 1 Samuel 17:40 we read that David picked up five smooth stones from a stream and put them into his shepherd's bag. Then, armed only with his shepherd's staff and a sling, he stepped out to fight the Philistine across the valley. Although the Bible does not clearly state why David took five stones or the meaning of each stone, I believe they represent the character of Christ within David, gleaned while tending sheep in a field alone with God. Therefore, David was provided all he needed to fight whatever giants came his way.

- **Love:** David's love for God and the people of God far outweighed any hate or rejection from the enemy.
- **Faith:** David's faith in God overcame any fear of the enemy.
- **Humility:** David's child-like faith in humility as a boy going before a giant with a sling shot and a rock cast down the spirit of pride.
- **Wisdom:** David's wisdom to not try wearing Saul's armor but to walk in his own God-given authority and identity from heaven overcame man's foolishness.
- **Joy:** David the worshiper found joy in the Lord's presence, overtaking a nation's sorrow.

Because David knew his identity in Christ, he could stand before a giant even though the mighty warriors of the land were shaking in their boots. A young boy named David was obedient to God.

Keep going when life points you toward the stepping stones—because with each stone there is a purpose and a plan written on the scrolls of heaven for you.

Trust in the Lord with all your heart; do not depend on your own understanding. Seek his will in all you do, and he will show you which path to take.

(Proverbs 3:5–6 NLT)

STUDY GUIDE

1 Samuel 17:40; Psalm 116:1–2; Hebrews 11:1; Psalm 116:6–16;
1 Samuel 16:7; 2 Samuel 7:18; 1 Samuel 16:14–23;
Psalm 22:1–26; 1 Chronicles 29:10–20; 1 Peter 5:5

PERSONAL REFLECTION

1. What are some of the stepping stones that have been on your pathway?
2. Have you stopped short of your destiny, or is there more God has in store for you?

JOY COMES IN THE MORNING

During some of the most challenging times of my life there have been some passages of the Bible I have not liked hearing! I only wanted to make it through quickly and survive the storm. After all, it's hard to have joy when you're in the midst of a trial!

Count it all joy when you fall into various trials,
knowing that the testing of your faith produces patience.
But let patience have its perfect work, that you may
be perfect and complete, lacking nothing.
(James 1:2–4 NKJV)

My character began growing amidst the storm when I finally realized what James 1:2–4 meant. I now know that God has a purpose and a plan for everything in my life. No matter what I face, God has provided a way out and is developing His character within me. And in that assurance I can find great joy.

Some of us haven't seen morning's joy for a long time. We're still stuck somewhere between darkness and twilight. So where is the joy? How can we have joy when the storm is raging all around us? Joy comes from knowing God's got you and from praising Him for it. Joy is walking in the peace of His love, keeping your eyes fixed on Jesus as you walk above the circumstances of life.

In Mark 4:35–41 we read that Jesus was sleeping in a boat when a fierce storm arose. Winds and waves tossed the boat about, and it began filling with water. The disciples, afraid that they would drown, woke Jesus with anxious shouts.

> *He arose and rebuked the wind, and said to the sea,*
> *"Peace, be still!" And the wind ceased and there*
> *was a great calm. But He said to them, "Why are*
> *you so fearful? How is it that you have no faith?"*
> (Mark 4:39–40 NKJV)

God strengthens us when we're weak when we allow Him to fill our hearts with joy by praising Him amidst the storm. There is always something we can praise Him for. When we take Him at His word and speak the name of Jesus, things change in the atmosphere. God's love and provision do not exempt us from trials but see us through them with peace.

> *You will keep in perfect peace all who trust in you,*
> *all whose thoughts are fixed on you!*
> (Isaiah 26:3 NLT)

> *Rejoice in your confident hope.*
> *Be patient in trouble, and keep on praying.*
> (Romans 12:12 NLT)

STUDY GUIDE

Psalm 30:5; Mark 4:35–41; Isaiah 40:29–31;
1 Peter 5:10; John 14:27

PERSONAL REFLECTION

1. Have trials robbed you of your joy? Journal your thoughts.
2. Are you willing to trust God and allow Him to build your character as you find joy in the peace that only He can give?

DRY GROUND

Have you ever waited with anticipation for something, only to be filled with disappointment when it arrived? It may have not come as expected or was not in the proper packaging. Life can be disappointing when we put our hope and trust in people and things rather than in a loving, caring God. Sometimes God's plan for our lives looks different than we have envisioned, thus taking us on an unexpected road trip of speed bumps and detours. And although it feels as if we are never making progress, God's plan for our life has not changed.

We read in the book of Exodus about Moses and Joshua, two faithful leaders who led the Israelites out of Egypt into the promised land, a different kind of journey than the Israelites had anticipated. And because the trip wasn't what the people had expected, they wandered around in the wilderness on dry ground for forty years. Feeling hopeless and forsaken, they complained about everything, forgetting the miracles God had performed for them.

We read in Exodus 14 that when the Egyptians chased the Israelites, God parted the waters so the Israelites could walk across on dry ground. That dry ground became the pathway to the promised land. However, when they came near the promised land, we are told in Numbers 14:6–10 that only Joshua and Caleb could see the truth of what was there. The others had become so blinded by their circumstances that their hearts had become too calloused to receive the truth. This highlights the crucial role of faith in perceiving God's plan, even in the midst of adversity.

When it looks as if we may drown amid the journey and the hopes and dreams God has placed in our hearts seem only to lead to dry places, we must trust God. We must trust that through it all, He is not just building our character but also transforming it. He sometimes provides speed bumps and detours to slow us down so we will make the right turn, and in doing so, He is shaping us into stronger, more resilient individuals. This is a powerful reminder to trust in God's plan, even when it seems to lead us through challenging and unexpected paths.

STUDY GUIDE

Proverbs 13:12; Exodus 14; Exodus 17:1–7; Numbers 20:2–13;
Exodus 14:11–22; Joshua 3:5–17; Ecclesiastes 3:11;
Matthew 13:15; Numbers 14:6–10; Exodus 16:2–3

PERSONAL REFLECTION

1. In what ways have complaining and fear caused you to be blinded to the provision of God in your life?
2. In what situations have you seen God's provision amidst the speed bumps and detours?

THE WILDERNESS JOURNEY

In Exodus 12:31–39 we witness the Israelites not leaving Egypt poor and helpless. On the contrary, they were very wealthy and needed nothing more to survive. They had more than they needed to build, grow, and prosper. We know they took almost ten thousand pounds of silver and gold and over five thousand pounds of bronze, which they used to create the tabernacle. In addition, God also provided the livestock for offerings; the wood, fabric, jewels, and other gold and silver used for Aaron's vest, the altar, and the lampstands.

God even gave the Israelites unique talents and abilities so they could accomplish what He had called them to do. God didn't provide them with quail because they needed it but rather because they wanted it! He supplied not only their needs but also their desires!

When the Israelites left Egypt they were not just taking away cheap labor from Pharaoh and the Egyptians—they were taking the wealth and riches of the land. They were taking the blessing of God with them.

In the desert during our wilderness journey, just like the Israelites, we tend to complain even though we have all we need to survive. But God has already supplied all we need for the journey. This "journey" is not just physical travel but also a spiritual pilgrimage, a process of growth, learning, and transformation. It is a journey of faith, where God's provision and guidance are always present, even in the most challenging times.

And amidst the battle, just as Aaron and Hur held up Moses' hands so the Israelites could win the battle, God has provided someone to stand with you to lift your arms in prayer in whatever battle you face.

"Behold, I send an Angel before you to keep you in the way and to bring you into the place I have prepared."

(Exodus 23:20 NKJV)

STUDY GUIDE

Exodus 12:35–36; Exodus 35; Exodus 28:2; Exodus 16:11–16;
Exodus 17:8–13; Isaiah 45:2–3; Psalm 105:37–45

PERSONAL REFLECTION

1. When has God provided someone to stand by you and believe for you in prayer?
2. Can you remember a time when you stood in the gap for someone else in prayer?

THE ROAD OF DESPAIR

In Luke 10:30–37 the situation looked grim for a Jewish man attacked by bandits—he had been robbed, beaten severely, and left for dead while traveling from Jerusalem to Jericho. A Jewish priest came along, and seeing the man lying on the road, he crossed to the other side and went on his way. Later, a religious man walked down the same route and crossed to the other side of the road without stopping. Finally, a Samaritan came upon the bleeding man. Being moved with a heart of compassion, the Samaritan treated the wounds of the Jewish traveler, put him on his donkey, and took him to an inn to be cared for and paid for all his expenses.

Each of us at times may have been able to relate to the man left by the side of the road wounded and bleeding, watching others go about their busy lives as we bleed from the pain that life has inflicted. We tend to isolate ourselves as a form of protection, yet we long for someone to reach out in compassion and love to help heal our wounded heart.

We all have our crosses to bear, but who's to say which cross is heavier? There are times when life can be overwhelming, such as when we're dealing with the worry and stress of finances, job loss, sickness, or the death of a loved one. Although we may handle life situations differently than our neighbors, that doesn't mean one cross weighs any less than the other.

Knowing that life would sometimes leave us bleeding and dying on a road of despair, Jesus, moved with a heart of compassion and love, provided a way to heal us by going to the cross. He paid the price with His blood so we could be free to live a life of peace amidst our circumstances.

There are times we are overwhelmed and don't know what to do. Others persecute us, but God has not forsaken us. And He has provided a way out for us through His Son, Jesus.

> *"Greater love has no man than this, than to*
> *lay down one's life for his friends."*
> (John 15:13 NKJV)

STUDY GUIDE
Luke 10:30–37; 2 Corinthians 4:7; Matthew 25:40

PERSONAL REFLECTION
1. Can you think of a time when God provided for you at just the right time?
2. How did it make you feel?

CAN YOU HEAR THE WHISPER?

In 1 Kings 19:1–15 we read that when Jezebel, the queen of Israel, threatened Elijah's life, burdened by fear, the prophet of God ran alone into the wilderness. At the end of the first day while resting under a tree, he prayed that he would die— and eventually fell asleep. But an angel of the Lord touched Elijah and told him to get up and eat to be strengthened for the journey ahead. So Elijah ate the food the angel had prepared, which gave him enough strength to travel for forty days to Mount Horeb, where he found a cave to spend the night. But the Lord asked Elijah, "What are you doing here? Go and stand before me on the mountain."

As Elijah stood there, a mighty windstorm hit the mountain, and afterward came an earthquake and a fire. The Lord was not in the wind, earthquake, or fire, but He passed by amidst it. When Elijah finally became still enough, he could hear the gentle whisper of God's instruction for him. And God told Elijah to go back the same way he had come through the wilderness of Damascus.

God knew where Elijah was going and why he was going. He even ensured that Elijah had food and water to strengthen him for the journey he was about to embark on. Overcome with fear, Elijah spent over eighty days traveling in the wilderness. God protected him amidst the mountain's wind, earthquake, and fire. When Elijah finally stopped and was no longer overcome by fear, he became quiet enough to hear the whisper of the Lord's voice.

The Spirit of the Lord remained with Elijah despite his fear and his temporary forgetfulness of his identity as a prophet of

God. Even though God had never left Elijah's side, He allowed him to go on the journey through the wilderness so that his faith and character would be strengthened. While providing for Elijah along the way, God let Elijah know that hearing the whisper of His voice is all about standing still and knowing that He is God.

Fear can cause us to make rash decisions, and just like Elijah, you may find that the wilderness is a place of testing and renewal. But it is not until we stop to listen for the whisper that we can hear God say, "Stop running—I've got this!"

*"Fear not, for I am with you; be not dismayed,
for I am your God; I will strengthen you, I will help you,
I will uphold you with my righteous right hand."*
(Isaiah 41:10 NKJV)

STUDY GUIDE
1 Kings 18–19; Philippians 4:6

PERSONAL REFLECTION
1. Has fear caused you to make foolish decisions?
2. Has God provided for you even when you have made foolish choices?

FALSE EVIDENCE APPEARING REAL

I've heard that fear is false evidence appearing real. Fear is known to cause physical, emotional, and spiritual problems. But when we choose faith over fear, it can transform our lives. Fear can cause anxiety; it can steal our joy and make us blind to God's apparent provision. But faith can overcome fear, allowing us to live in spiritual freedom, with the knowledge that God has a divine plan and purpose for our lives.

In Genesis 21:8–21 we read about Hagar, who was sent away with her son, Ishmael, by her husband, Abraham. She was wandering in the wilderness with all their water gone. So Hagar set the boy in the shade of a shrub. She then sat a distance away so she would not have to watch her son die. But God heard her cry for help and sent an angel to Hagar. The angel asked Hagar what was wrong and told her not to be afraid, to comfort her son. Then God opened her eyes, and she saw a well full of water. She filled her water container and gave her son a drink. Mother and son lived the in wilderness, and God was with the boy as he grew up. He became a skillful archer and married a woman from Egypt.

I believe that the fear of watching her child die and dying herself in the wilderness caused Hagar to become blind to God's provision. The scripture clearly states in Genesis 21:19 that God opened Hagar's eyes, and she saw the well full of water. The well of provision was there all the time because God had already gone ahead of Hagar and had prepared the way.

Many times what we see through the eyes of fear are lies we have come to believe. When our eyes are opened and the veil is lifted, we can see clearly that God's provision for us has been there all along, a constant presence in our lives, ready to comfort and sustain us.

> *"The Lord, He is the One who goes before you.*
> *He will be with you, He will not leave you nor*
> *forsake you; do not fear nor be dismayed."*
>
> (Deuteronomy 31:8 (NKJV)

STUDY GUIDE
Genesis 21:8–21; Psalms 37:25

PERSONAL REFLECTION
1. Has fear blinded you from the provision of God?
2. Give an example.

A JAR OF OIL

The spirit of lack, borne from the residue of past experience, lingers among us like a virus. We get caught up in discouragement rather than encouraging ourselves in the Lord.

In 2 Kings 4:1–7 we read how God provided for a destitute widow and her two sons. Her sons were being taken by her creditors as slaves to pay for the debt their mother owed. Trusting God for the outcome, the widow went humbly yet boldly to the prophet Elisha for guidance. When Elisha asked the widow what she had in her house, she replied that she had one jar of oil. At this, Elisha instructed her to gather as many empty containers as she could and pour what little oil she had into each container. Stepping out in faith, believing God would supply her needs, the woman filled multiple containers to the brim with one jar of oil. The oil stopped multiplying once there were no containers left to fill. Elisha then instructed her to sell the oil to pay her debt and to keep what was left for the future needs of her family.

Despite her dire circumstances, the widow displayed remarkable courage. She recognized her identity as a child of God and boldly sought guidance from the man of God. Her actions serve as a powerful reminder that we too are children of God. When faced with advice that may seem illogical, we can take a leap of faith, knowing that our heavenly Father will always provide for His children.

Trusting in God, seeking wise counsel, and obeying His instruction are not just principles but practical steps we can take in times of need. The same God who multiplied the oil for the widow stands ready to provide for us. Sometimes we must step out in faith and use what we have. This practical lesson reminds us that we too can trust in God's provision and seek His guidance in our times of need.

"Look at the birds of the air, for they neither sow nor reap nor gather into barns; yet your heavenly Father feeds them. Are you not of more value than they?"

(Matthew 6:26 NKJV)

STUDY GUIDE

James 4:2–3; 1 Samuel 30:6; 2 Kings 4:1–7;
Proverbs 12:15; Matthew 6:25–27; Psalm 37:25

PERSONAL REFLECTION

1. Can you humble yourself to admit your need?
2. Write your prayer request here as you pray, asking God for wisdom.

ILLEGAL ENTRY

There may be moments when we feel inadequate, alone, or unimportant. We might question our worth, our age, or our qualifications. But in those times, remember—God has not abandoned us. He loves us unconditionally. Every aspect of our lives matters to Him. He is deeply invested in what and who we care about.

Let me remind you of a boy named David, whom we read about in 1 Samuel 17:24–37. When others saw a giant, David saw an opportunity. The boy appeared to have no armor, weapons of magnitude, or sense. When the army of God was shaking in their boots in fear of the Philistines, David stood before the giant and said, "How dare you defile the army of the living God?" The principality of darkness had overstepped the boundary line of the kingdom of heaven, where David knew God had established his citizenship. He was able to stand against a giant without fear. David didn't need anyone to remind him about the provision of his God.

When we know to whom we belong and our legal rights as citizens of the kingdom of heaven, we can stand against any giant in the land. Jesus overcame the tribulations of this world on the cross by the blood He shed and the price He paid. Therefore, anything less than the promise of the Word of God is illegal entry into our lives!

While we navigate a fallen world, a realm where Satan dwells, we are not left defenseless. As children of God, we possess a secure identity. We can confront adversity with unwavering faith, knowing that our God has gone before us, equipping us with everything we need to overcome life's challenges.

"These things I have spoken to you, that in Me you may have peace. In the world you will have tribulation; but be of good cheer, I have overcome the world."

(John 16:33 NKJV)

STUDY GUIDE

1 Samuel 17:24–37; 1 John 5:19; Philippians 1:27; Luke 12:7; Isaiah 53:5–6; 1 John 3:1–3

PERSONAL REFLECTION

1. What giants are you facing in your life?
2. As you step out into your God-given identity as a child of God, what is happening in your life that is illegal against a child of God?

LIFE APPLICATION

Father, I thank you that no matter where I am going or what is happening in my life, you have already gone before me and prepared the way. Thank you that fear and anxiety have no place in my life. Please help me to recognize the times I may have taken your provision for granted in my life. God, open my eyes that I might see, my ears that I might hear, and my heart that I might receive. Please help me to worry less and trust you more. Help my faith to grow from this moment on as I step out into the future, because I know that you have engraved my name on the palm of your hand. Thank you for loving and caring for me so profoundly.

In your name I pray.

Amen

7
IDENTITY

Discovering God's Plan for Your Life

IDENTITY: INTRODUCTION

Gold is found within the dust of the earth, which was spoken into existence by the voice of God. I believe gold was in the dust that day when God created man. Thus, gold dust must have been in the hand of God when He created a woman from the rib of man.

When God created you, He saw the finished product before your life began. He started from the end and worked backward, placing within you all the gold dust and gems you needed to complete your God-given assignment on earth while being seated with Him in heaven. Then He sat down in the place of rest, patiently waiting for you to join Him there so He could reveal His plans to you.

Although aware that God had a purpose and a plan for my life, I did not know my true value in Him, because I did not value myself. I have spent years trying to forget the distorted things I had believed to be true.

Through spending much time in prayer, fasting, and the Word of God, I found His character beginning to develop within me along the way. The closer I got to God, the revelation of His Word became clearer and He became my greatest passion as I longed to know Him better. It is there I began to discover my true value and identity in Him, of who He created me to be, a child of the most high God.

When the time was right, God brought the most amazing spiritual leaders into my life who saw the value of God within me. And as I submitted myself to their leadership, by the direction of Holy Spirit within them they have guided me on an incredible journey of discovering who God called me to be.

I pray that the person of the Holy Spirit will place within you a longing to draw deeply from the wells of His love for you and that your spiritual eyes will be opened as you read this chapter on the journey of discovering the gems God has placed within you. I pray you will begin to see yourself through the eyes of your heavenly Father as you cross over the Jordan and realize your true God-given identity in Him. May the realization of God's love for you permeate your soul as you draw close to Him and He reveals the treasure hidden within His Word for you.

INSUFFICIENT

A story in John 6:1–13 of a young boy has been told countless times throughout history. We don't know his name or how old he was. We only know that he came prepared to see Jesus, prepared for the time he was going to be where Jesus was, with a heart to serve and to share what little he had.

When Jesus crossed over to the far side of the Sea of Galilee, a huge crowd followed Him. So He climbed a hill and sat down with His disciples around Him. Then He turned to Phillip and asked, "Where can we buy food to feed all these people?" Jesus was testing Phillip because Jesus already knew what He was going to do.

Phillip replied, "We don't have enough money to feed them!"

Then Andrew spoke up: "There's a young boy here with five loaves of bread and two fish. But that's not near enough to feed such a crowd."

"Tell everyone to sit down," Jesus said, so they all sat down. Then Jesus took the bread and the fish and gave thanks. After the food had been distributed, five thousand men and their families ate until full, and there were twelve baskets of food left over.

How blessed this young boy must have been to give his food to Jesus! How excited he must have been when Jesus multiplied what little he had and fed so many people! The boy and the amount of food in proportion to the number of people seemed insignificant. But there was more than enough food and plenty of leftovers!

You may feel insignificant, and your name may not be well

known. You may feel you haven't much to give. But all you need is a heart to be with Jesus—because you are significant to Him! And that's all that matters.

> *"The things which are impossible with*
> *men are possible with God."*
> (Luke 18:27 NKJV)

STUDY GUIDE

John 6:1–13; 1 Samuel 16:7; Jeremiah 29:11

PERSONAL REFLECTION

1. Have you been afraid to offer to Jesus what you have because you feel it's insignificant?
2. In what way has God used for His glory something you thought insignificant?

WHAT'S IN YOUR HAND?

When God created us, He had a purpose and plan for our lives. He gave us everything we needed to walk in it. Therefore, we must realize that our calling is not what we do but who we are. We waste our energy comparing ourselves to others and fail to look within the vault of treasures God has placed within us.

In Matthew 25:14–30 Jesus told a story about a wealthy man who went on a trip. Before he left, he called his servants together. The man gave five talents of silver to one, two to another, and one to the last. He distributed the talents in proportion to their abilities. While he was gone, the man who had received five talents invested them, thus doubling the amount to ten. The man given two talents also doubled that amount. But the man who received one talent dug a hole and buried it because he feared losing the money.

After a while the wealthy man returned home. When he asked the servants what they had done with the talents he had given them, he found that the man to whom he had given one talent had buried it in the ground while the other two had doubled the amounts they were given. He was pleased with the two who had invested their money, but he was displeased with the man who had buried his in the ground. Therefore, he took the talent from the one who had buried it and gave it to the man with ten talents.

We can begin discovering the treasure of our identity in Christ by using what we have. What's in your hand?

- Moses had a staff in his hand, and he went from a basket floating in a river to a king's palace to become the leader of a nation.
- David had a staff, a sling, a harp, and a sword in his hand at various times throughout his lifetime. He went from a field of sheep to a king's palace, onto a battlefield, and to a king's throne.
- Elisha had a plow and oxen in his hand; he went from a farmer's field to being a prophet's assistant to being a prophet of double portion.
- Joseph had a shepherd's staff in his hand, and he went from being a shepherd to a pit, to a prison—to being in charge of the entire land of Egypt.

Whatever God's plan for our lives is, it begins with what He has placed in our hands. God's plan for your life is as unique as He made you to be. And He has put everything in you to accomplish what He has called you to do.

"His lord said to him, 'Well done, good and faithful servant; you have been faithful over a few things, I will make you ruler over many things. Enter into the joy of your lord.'"
(Matthew 25:23 NKJV)

STUDY GUIDE

Matthew 25:14–30; Galatians 6:4; Ecclesiastes 3:1–8;
Exodus 2:1–10; Exodus 4:17; Exodus 1:2–2:23; Acts 7:20-22;
1 Samuel 17:34–37; 1 Samuel 16:14–23; 1 Samuel 17:50–53;
2 Samuel 6:1; 2 Samuel 5:4; 1 Kings 19:19–21; 2 Kings 2:9–15;
Genesis 37:1–4; Genesis 37:23–28; Genesis 39:20–23;
Genesis 41:41–46

PERSONAL REFLECTION

1. What is in your hand?
2. Ask God how you can use what's in your hand to glorify Him. Journal your thoughts.

ONE STITCH AT A TIME

God had a plan for your life before He formed you in the womb. All the delicate inner parts of your body were knit together in your mother's womb by the hand of God. You were carefully planned out and made so wonderfully complex, and only one of you exists. No one else can replace God's plan for your life. God watched you as you were being formed and woven together in the dark of the womb. This is a testament to His guidance and care for you.

When a person knits an article of clothing, each thread of yarn is pulled through individually. When another color of yarn is added to the garment, the new color must be knitted in with the existing yarn and then knitted into the garment. If that color of yarn doesn't match the color scheme of what is being made, it will be noticeable and will not fit into the finished pattern. Or while knitting something, if you decide to change the design of the stitch from the one you have been using, it will show up in your final project. And if while knitting a garment you accidentally miss a stitch, the result will be a hole in your project. If the pattern and instructions are not followed carefully, your garment will not turn out correctly.

You made all the delicate, inner parts of my body
and knit me together in my mother's womb.
(Psalm 139:13 NLT)

Before you were born, God knit you together in your mother's womb, one thread, weave, pattern, and color at a time. This is a testament to how much God loves you and how uniquely you are designed. He never chose a design, stitch, or color that didn't match who you are. He never made a mistake or missed a stitch, leaving holes in His plan for your life—because you were perfectly designed by the hand of God, created in His image and for His glory.

We have all made mistakes and choices we're not proud of. And we may have suffered the consequences of those choices by allowing the wrong people or things into our lives only to end up with a hole in our hearts, finances, or future.

Although we may try to fix things, the damage in many situations has been done. And the only one who can truly improve what we messed up is God Himself. Just as a hand-knitted garment with mistakes in it can be fixed if knitted correctly by the master's hands, our lives can be restored and renewed through the power of God's grace and our faith in Him. It is through this faith that we can find the strength and guidance to move forward in His plan for us.

"When you pass through the waters, I will be with you; and through the rivers, they shall not overflow you. When you walk through the fire, you shall not be burned, nor shall the flame scorch you."

(Isaiah 43:2 NKJV)

STUDY GUIDE

Jeremiah 1:5; Psalm 139:13–16; Jeremiah 31:3;
1 Corinthians 10:13

PERSONAL REFLECTION

1. Has life left you with holes in your heart?
2. Have there been parts of your life that only the Master's hand can fix?

THE ORIGINAL DESIGN

When a qualified carpenter builds a house, he doesn't just go out, get some wood, and start building. He strategically plans for the finished project. He lays out the blueprint while collecting the right tools and equipment needed for the job. At the same time, he seeks out people with the talent to complete other areas of the project. But before the carpenter can build a house and knows exactly how it should be done, he must be trained and equipped by someone who has gone before and accomplished the vision set before them—an instructor, a master of the craft who has schooled himself or herself in knowledge and experience in the building profession.

God, the master creator, has uniquely fashioned you in His image, making you special and significant. He has a specific, tailor-made plan for your life that only you can fulfill. You are not a mere copy but an original creation, birthed in God's heart and formed by His hand. He has equipped you with the desire and talent to accomplish everything in His plan. As the master carpenter, He will guide you to discover the treasure He has placed in you. But you must position your heart in the place where He is. Study His blueprint for your life in His love letter to you, the Bible. And choose to surround yourself with people who will encourage your walk with God.

We were all created with the need to belong, to be valued, and to be accepted. The need for acceptance can lead us toward God and His designed plan for our lives, which brings fulfillment and purpose. On the other hand, the need for acceptance can lead us down a path of self-destruction as we copy the behavior and customs of the world around us, which brings emptiness and despair. The choice is ours. We can choose whether to accept and embrace God's plan for our lives or to follow a path that leads to self-destruction. This choice is a vital part of our faith journey, and through this choice we can find fulfillment in Christ.

When a fashion designer creates an original design, the copyright belongs to him or her. Anything like it is considered a knockoff, which is an unauthorized copy or imitation of the actual product. The design is made quickly and easily, which lowers the product's value. However, the original design is of high value.

Satan is a copycat. He wants to destroy all that God has put within you by leading you down a pathway of destruction. Have you ever looked up the definition of destruction? Destruction is an action or process to cause so much damage to something that it no longer exists or cannot be repaired, the method of killing something (Webster).

"The thief does not come except to steal, and to kill, and to destroy. I have come that they may have life, and that they may have it more abundantly."
(John 10:10 NKJV)

You are not a mere imitation but a unique creation for whom God has a distinct plan. There is no one else like you, and the plan for your life is one of a kind. It may resemble someone else's plan, but it is tailored to you, like a shoe custom-made for your foot. You hold a special place in God's heart; He loves you so deeply that He sacrificed His Son so you could walk in the freedom of His original plan for your life. You are not just a part of His plan—you are the focal point of His love and attention. Your uniqueness is not a mistake but a testament to God's creativity and love for you.

It's not too late! I encourage you to begin renewing your mind today by changing your thoughts. Your value is not based on what others think of you. It is based on what God says about you in His Word. This process of renewing the mind involves consciously aligning our thoughts with God's truth and rejecting negative thoughts. It is a powerful tool that helps us better understand and embrace God's blueprint for our lives.

Do not be conformed to this world, but be transformed by the renewing of your mind, that you may prove what is that good and acceptable and perfect will of God.

(Romans 12:2 NKJV)

STUDY GUIDE

Genesis 1:1; Genesis 1:27; Genesis 1:26–27; Jeremiah 29:11;
Romans 12:6; 2 Timothy 3:17; 1 Peter 5:6; John 10:29;
Isaiah 41:10; Psalm 32:8; 1 Corinthians 15:33;
Hebrews 10:24–25; 1 Thessalonians 5:11; John 3:16

PERSONAL REFLECTION

1. Do you believe God has an original blueprint for your life?
2. In what ways might you discover what is written on the blueprint of your life?

SOMEONE ELSE'S SHOES

I love shoes, and I love shopping for shoes. But a shoe that does not fit my foot correctly is very uncomfortable. In the same way, when we try to fit into roles or expectations that are not meant for us, it can be spiritually uncomfortable. Although some shoes are my size, they sometimes feel bad on my feet. And let me be honest—I am not attracted to every style of shoe. Similarly, we may not resonate with every aspect of our spiritual journey. The most comfortable shoes become the most worn shoes, just as embracing our true selves and our unique spiritual path can bring the most fulfillment.

Children love walking around in their parents' shoes, even though the shoes are way too big and awkward for them. They enjoy pretending they fit. Although pretending is cute when a young child does it, it is not appealing when it occurs in the body of Christ, which refers to the community of believers. After all, how can one function correctly if his or her shoes do not fit properly? This metaphor emphasizes the importance of embracing our unique roles and gifts within the spiritual community.

Our bodies have many parts, and God has put each part just where he wants it. How strange a body would be if it had only one part!
(1 Corinthians 12:18–19 NLT)

The body has many parts, yet it is one body. If the elbow says, "I am not part of the body because I am not a knee," it is no less a part of the body. And if the heart valve says, "I am not a part of the body because I am not outwardly seen," does that make it any less a part of the body? If the whole body were a mouth, how would we hear? There are many parts to the human body, and God has put each piece right where He wants it. The elbow cannot say to the knee, "I don't need you." All parts of the body are required to function correctly. Some features of the body that seem the least significant are the most necessary. This metaphor of the body emphasizes the importance of every individual's unique contribution to the spiritual community.

Imagine your ear trying to walk down the street. Or imagine depending on your elbow for every breath you take. How about your stomach pumping the blood through your foot? Or is your mouth trying to listen and hear for you? Although these thoughts may seem ridiculous, we continually compare ourselves to others, wishing we had the talent to sing, speak, teach, paint, or play the piano as someone else does. Yet for some reason, we think less of the gifts in our lives than those others seem to possess.

Our imagination can run away with us or be one of the most valuable gifts we have ever received. Imagine yourself as more than enough rather than less than. Imagine having all the tools, talents, and grace you need. Imagine walking in shoes that fit you perfectly, made by the hand of God just for you.

We each have specific characteristics, some of which we were born with, some we develop as we grow, and others we have yet to discover. But we all carry something unique that no one else has. The road map to finding who God created you to be is time spent alone with the God who made you.

Stop comparing yourself to others and start being the best you can be. Stop trying to walk in the shoes that belong to someone else. They don't fit you because you have yet to travel the same road or fight the same battles to get where they are. Humans are never satisfied—we want what others have, whether a position, material things, or specific skills. But when we take our eyes off people and put our eyes on Jesus, we will see things differently. Focus on your own journey and the unique path that God has laid out for you.

One and the same Spirit works all these things,
distributing to each one individually as He wills.
(1 Corinthians 12:11 NKJV)

STUDY GUIDE
1 Corinthians 12:12–22; Romans 12:4–8

PERSONAL REFLECTION

1. Have you ever compared yourself to someone else?
2. Give an example of when you tried walking in someone else's shoes.

KINGDOM IDENTITY

What is a kingdom? A kingdom is a government or a country headed by a king or queen; a realm, a domain, or a territory, such as the spiritual realm of God. In a kingdom there is a constitution or a covenant between the king and the citizens. There are principles by which it functions (Webster).

Scripture reveals to us that our citizenship is not just in any kingdom, but in the heavenly kingdom. As citizens, we can legally obtain the keys to the kingdom of heaven. Jesus Himself declared, "I will give you the keys to the kingdom of heaven." This is a privilege and honor that sets His children apart.

"Whatever you bind on earth will be bound in heaven, and whatever you loose on earth will be loosed in heaven."

(Matthew 16:19 NKJV)

If I give you the keys to my home, I have given you authority to access my home. And if you have access to my home, you can access what is in my home. The keys in this verse represent God's delegated authority.

Above all, you must live as citizens of heaven.

(Philippians 1:27 NLT)

We sometimes forget or have never realized that we are citizens of the kingdom of heaven. When we understand who we are, we will know what we can access because we have rights to everything in the Father's house. "The enemy is not threatened by what you do. His greatest fear is that you will discover who you are and begin to walk in your God-given identity as a son or daughter of the King. But nothing is yours until you understand it. Therefore, we must change the way we think because what we think will take root in our hearts if allowed. And what we meditate on will be deposited into our spirit. The kingdom of God resides in your heart. This is why we are told in Scripture to be diligent about guarding our hearts. Our conscious mind feeds on our subconscious mind, which is our heart. And whatever controls our mind controls our heart" (Apostle Dr. Marshall McGee).

"My people are destroyed for lack of knowledge."
(Hosea 4:6 NKJV)

Therefore, the transformation of our mind can catapult us into our kingdom identity. The choice is up to each one of us—because our inheritance as children of God is there for the taking.

"Seek first the kingdom of God and His righteousness, and all these things shall be added to you."
(Matthew 6:33 NKJV)

STUDY GUIDE

Philippians 3:20; Philippians 1:27; Proverbs 23:7;
Matthew 22:1–14; Philippians 3:20

PERSONAL REFLECTION

1. Do you believe you have dual citizenship in heaven and on earth?
2. How might your life change if you began living as a citizen of heaven while still on earth?

_____

_____

_____

_____

_____

_____

_____

_____

_____

_____

_____

_____

_____

_____

_____

_____

_____

_____

_____

OUR INHERITANCE

We live in a world of lost identity. People are trying to find themselves in a fallen world. And without Jesus and the revelation of Him, that's impossible. The spirit of confusion permeates the earth as Christians and non-Christians continue believing the lies about themselves they have become accustomed to. At the same time, gravitation toward the familiar becomes a vicious circle.

Until we embrace Jesus and His love for us, we will never know what God wrote on the scrolls of heaven about us, and we will never know the revelation of our true identity in Him, which is a part of our inheritance as His children. Confusion is not of God. He never intended for you, His creation, to live in a false identity, never knowing who He created you to be.

Jesus came so He could get His life back into us. And with that comes the inheritance of the Father to His children. Therefore, as we pursue a relationship with our heavenly Father, His character will be developed in us. And we will think differently as our minds are transformed into the newness of Him.

When we realize our true identity in Christ, we will be unstoppable as we take hold of our inheritance as children of the highest God.

God's heart is overflowing with blessings for us, and we have direct access to It. Everything God has had in store for us since the beginning of time, including His boundless love, unmerited grace, and abundant blessings, is in His heart for us. Therefore, we have the privilege to seek out the hidden treasure within us through the written Word of God.

I encourage you to draw near to God through prayer, reading the Bible, and fellowship with other believers. Seek what is in His heart for you by meditating on His Word and asking for His guidance in prayer so that He will reveal and unlock the treasure hidden within you to glorify Him on earth.

God decided in advance to adopt us into his own family by bringing us to himself through Jesus Christ. This is what he wanted to do, and it gave him great pleasure.

(Ephesians 1:5 NLT)

STUDY GUIDE

Psalm 139:16; Matthew 7:11; 1 Corinthians 15:45–49;
Genesis 2:7; Romans 12:2; Isaiah 40:13; John 4:4–26;
Genesis 1:27–2:7; John 10:10; Romans 12:2; Matthew 5:13–14;
Jeremiah 1:5; Hebrews 10:16–25; John 1:11–13

PERSONAL REFLECTION

1. Ask the Holy Spirit to awaken you to your God-given identity and purpose on the earth.
2. Do you know all that you have access to in heaven through your adoption by Him?

A NEW NAME

In Genesis 25:21–26 we are told of twin brothers who battled in stubborn competition while in the womb. I can only imagine what their childhood must have been like, in constant contention with one another, which extended into adulthood.

Life at times can leave us fearful of the future. For Jacob, it was the fear of rejection and possibly losing his life in a battle with his older brother, Esau, from whom he had stolen the firstborn birthright.

After Jacob had worked for his father-in-law, Laban, for several years and was cheated out of most of his earnings, God told him to return to Canaan, the land from which he came, where his brother, Esau, lived. So Jacob packed up his family and possessions and started on his journey. Jacob, afraid that his brother, Esau, would take revenge on him for stealing the firstborn birthright years earlier, sent his family and possessions ahead with gifts for his brother, Esau, thus leaving Jacob alone in the camp, where an angel came and wrestled with him during the night. At daylight the angel, seeing that he could not defeat Jacob, struck Jacob's hip and put it out of joint. Then the angel told Jacob to let him go. But Jacob refused to let go until the angel blessed him. So the angel blessed him and said to him, "Your name will no longer be 'Jacob' but 'Israel,' because you have wrestled with God and with man, and you have won." After a sleepless night, limping as he walked, Jacob continued his journey to meet his brother, Esau.

Jacob's struggle with God and man that night in the camp symbolized the battle with his inner self. God wanted Jacob to admit that he was weak and afraid and that although he had spent many years serving his father-in-law, Laban, a deceitful trickster, Jacob himself was a trickster as well. He did not win the battle against God that night but rather against the flesh within himself.

Although Jacob had received the firstborn inheritance from his earthly father, he still needed to be fulfilled. Jacob's life was far from peaceful; he lived in guilt, shame, and fear as he continued reaping what he had sown. The battle that took place in the camp that night was worth the transformation that took place in Jacob's mind and was also worth walking with a limp for the remainder of his life. When Jacob came face to face with the Spirit of God amidst his fear, he also had to face the nature within himself and make peace with God at that moment.

The encounter in the camp that night, where Jacob came away walking with a limp, served only to remind him that he had experienced the separation of flesh and spirit, thus giving him a clear vision to walk in the true identity of who God had created him to be: "Israel," the father of many nations.

Even before he made the world, God loved us and chose us in Christ to be holy and without fault in his eyes. God decided in advance to adopt us into his own family by bringing us to himself through Jesus Christ. This is what he wanted to do, and it gave him great pleasure.

(Ephesians 2:4–5 NLT)

STUDY GUIDE

Hosea 12:3–5; Genesis 26:21–26; Genesis 31:3;
Genesis 31–33:16; 2 Timothy 3:16–17

PERSONAL REFLECTION

1. In what way might you be wrestling between your flesh and your spirit?
2. Are you willing to give up your plans for God's plans?

STEPS TO DISCOVERING YOUR
GOD-GIVEN IDENTITY

- Believe God's Word. When we neglect the Word of God, we ignore the very thing that can change our life.

    "You will know the truth, and the truth will set you free" (John 8:32 NLT).

- Love the Lord with all your heart, soul, and mind.

    "'You must love the Lord your God with all your heart, all your soul, all your mind, and all your strength'" (Mark 12:30 NLT).

- Spend time with the God who created you—through worship, prayer, Bible study, and listening for His voice.

    "When you pray, go away by yourself, shut the door behind you, and pray to your Father in private. Then your Father, who sees everything, will reward you" (Matthew 6:6 NLT).

- Change the way you think. Stop believing lies about yourself, others, and things.

    Don't copy the behavior and customs of this world, but let God transform you into a new person by changing the way you think. Then you will learn to know God's will for you, which is good and pleasing and perfect (Romans 12:2 NLT).

- Ask God to increase your faith. If you have confidence in God and His Word, use what you have so that it will grow.

    "If you had faith even as small as a mustard seed, you could say to this mulberry tree, 'May you be uprooted and be

planted in the sea,' and it would obey you!" (Luke 17:6 NLT).

- Stop letting fear dictate your life.

  God has not given us a spirit of fear and timidity, but of power, love, and self-discipline (2 Timothy 1:7 NLT).

- Ask God for direction and guidance. He will order and guide your steps as you allow Him to.

  If you need wisdom, ask our generous God, and he will give it to you. He will not rebuke you for asking. But when you ask him, be sure that your faith is in God alone (James 1:5–6 NLT).

- Step out in faith and use what you have.

  We walk by faith, not by sight (2 Corinthians 5:7 NKJV).

- Surround yourself with people who will encourage you in your walk with God.

  Bad company corrupts good character (1 Corinthians 15:33 NLT).

- Seek wise biblical counsel. Ask God to lead you to someone who lives a godly life and can guide you by the Word of God.

  A wise man will hear and increase learning, and a man of understanding will attain wise counsel (Proverbs 1:5 NKJV).

- Let Holy Spirit set your boundaries, and start trusting Him instead of yourself.

  Trust in the Lord with all your heart; do not depend on

your own understanding. Seek his will in all you do, and he will show you which path to take (Proverbs 3:5–6 NLT).

"Seek the Kingdom of God above all else, and live righteously, and he will give you everything you need."
(Matthew 6:33 NLT)

STUDY GUIDE

Psalm 119:105; 2 Timothy 3:16; Mark12:30–31; John 4:23;
James 4:8; Jeremiah 29:13; Romans 12:2; Luke 17:5–6;
2 Timothy 1:7; John 16:13; Psalm 119:133; Philippians 4:6–7;
1 Corinthians 5:7; Proverbs 13:20; Hebrews 10:25;
Proverbs 1:5; Psalm 1:1; Hebrews 11:1; Matthew 6:33

PERSONAL REFLECTION

1. Do you seek wise, godly counsel?
2. Are you willing to let the Holy Spirit guide you into a deeper revelation of what that means?

LIFE APPLICATION

Thank you, Father, that you had a plan for my life since the beginning of time and that you have always seen the treasure within me. Open my eyes so that I can see, my ears so that I can hear, and my heart so that I can receive the revelation of who you created me to be on earth. Stir up the gold you have put within me so I might pour it onto others for your glory. Please help me not to get frustrated as you build my character. Help me to walk in faith, knowing that when the time is right, you will reveal and polish the gemstones you have placed within me. Help me position my heart in a place of rest with you while I wait. Thank you, Lord, for loving me and being patient with me. Thank you for the stepping stones leading me across the Jordan to discover my true identity in you.

Amen

GEMS IN THE SAND

I am but a pebble upon the sand
a grain within the master's hand
A tiny speck within the sea
in a world where there's only one of me
What purpose is there in the master plan
to place me here, within the sand?
With a sea of people surrounding me,
Oh, show me, God, what you planned to be
One tiny speck from a master plan
He holds me tight in His hand
He sees a purpose just for me
of how He planned it all to be
I look for an answer amidst the sound
of all the people gathered round
But then, in a whisper, I hear His voice
My child, for me, you must make a choice
A ripple effect I call you to
as my Word is renewed within you
sit with me, lean on my chest
as I reveal to you the place of rest
A place where you can live today
it is not so far away
just trust my Word
and give me your heart
my love for you will never part
Give to me what's in your hand
so I may do as I have planned
my treasured one, my precious jewel
for in you is all I've called you to

—Kathleen VonSeggern

CONCLUSION

In many situations I have been where you are. But more importantly, Jesus has been where you are. His understanding and empathy are boundless, and He can relate to you on all levels. I share not just parts but significant moments of my story, so you will know that this book is Bible teaching and a reflection of my journey. I have carefully chosen scripture, stories, and biblical characters that I profoundly relate to and have spoken to me throughout the years. Although I have referred to some biblical characters more than once, there is still much to learn from them.

God hides levels of truth from us until we are hungry and thirsty for it. Therefore, we must diligently search it out within the Word of God because revelation must be discovered just as treasured gems are mined for.

It is the glory of God to conceal a matter, But the glory of kings to search out a matter.
(Proverbs 25:2 NKJV)

As you mine for the jewels of the kingdom within the Word of God and discover the jewel you are to Him, remember that this journey is ongoing. It's a journey filled with blessings and challenges, but it's a journey that leads to a deeper relationship with Christ. I pray that you have been blessed and will continue to pursue this relationship, unwavering against all odds. As you discover the unique gifts, talents, and purpose that God has placed in you and the wisdom, guidance, and comfort that the Word of God holds for you, may you be inspired to keep moving forward.

SCRIPTURE REFERENCES

1. LOVE
There's Plenty to Go Around

Introduction
Psalm 105:5

From Head to Toe
Isaiah 53:3–5; Mark 15:15–20; John 3:16

Listen for the Heartbeat
2 Corinthians 6:18; Psalm 139:16; 1 John 4:9–10; John 13:23; John 21:15–17

The Universal Language
Romans 8:38–39; John 3:16; John 3:16–17; 1 Corinthians 13:4–7; Isaiah 53

For the Love of God
Mark 12:30–31; Matthew 7:20–23; Romans 9:20; Mark 15:15–20; John 3:16; 1 John 4:15–20

My Father's Eyes
Mark 8:22–25; 1 Samuel 16:4–13; Isaiah 64:8; 1 Samuel 16:4–13

Rejected by Man
Luke 5:12–16; Matthew 8:1–3; Psalm 147:3; Romans 8:38–39

A New Way to Love
1 John 4:16; John 4:23–24; John 18:10; Mark 3:13–16; John 21:15–19; Mark 12:30–34

Broken Vessel
Matthew 6:19–21; Luke 7:36–50; John 11:2; Luke 10:38–42; Romans 5:6–11

Sweating Blood

Mark 14:34; Isaiah 49:16; Luke 22:44; Genesis 2:7; 1 John 4:10; Jeremiah 31:3; Philippians 4:6–7

There's Always Room for More

Matthew 18:1–6; Malachi 3:17; Matthew 10:14; Matthew 7:6; Ephesians 4:11–16; Matthew 19:13–14; John 5:19

2. PRAYER
Stop Defying Gravity

Introduction

Luke 5:16; 1 John 5:7–12; John 14:19–31; Ephesians 5:22–23; Jeremiah 33:3; 1 Thessalonians 5:17

Teach Us to Pray

Matthew 6:7–13; James 5:16; Psalm 150:6; Romans 8:28; Philippians 4:19; Matthew 6:14–15; 1 Corinthians 10:13; Psalm 103:1–5

Hearing His Voice

1 Samuel 3:1–10; John 10:27; 1 Kings 19:11–12; Psalm 139:13–14; Philippians 4:8; Matthew 10:29–31; 1 Kings 19:11–12; Psalm 46:10; John 10:1–16

"Instant God"

Matthew 22:37; Matthew 5:45; John 16:33; Psalm 19:14; Luke 10:38–42; Psalm 46:10; Isaiah 40:31

What Is Prayer?

Jeremiah 29:13; 1 Thessalonians 5:16–18; Matthew 11:28–30; Psalm 55:17; Psalm 42:1; Ephesians 6:18

Posture Your Heart

Luke 10:38–42; John 4:23–24; Isaiah 29:11–13; Psalm 119:10–11

The Heart of Prayer

1 Timothy 4:7–8; Isaiah 29:13; Psalm 119:10–11; Galatians 6:9; John 13:23; Daniel 6:10; Ephesians 2:6; Isaiah 26:9; James 4:6–8; Luke 10:38–42; John 4:23–24; John 3:23–24; Luke 18:10–14

Intimacy with God

Matthew 6:9; 1 Peter 5:7; Psalm 82:6; Psalm 139:13–15; Genesis 18:23–33; Exodus 32:30; Psalm 143:5; 1 Samuel 17:32–37; Daniel 6:10–28; Luke 2:42–49; Philippians 1:6

Come Up a Little Higher

Ephesians 2:6; Matthew 6:9–10; 1 Corinthians 2:10; Proverbs 23:7; Revelation 4:1

From Heaven to Earth

Matthew 6:33; Matthew 16:19; Proverbs 23:7; Jeremiah 29:13; Matthew 7:7; Philippians 1:27; Philippians 3:17–20; Matthew 16:19; Ephesians 2:6–7

Jesus, Our Example

Luke 3:21–22; Luke 6:12–17; Mark 6:35–44; Luke 9:18–22; Luke 9:28–36; Luke 11:1–4; John 11:40–44; Matthew 26:26; Luke 22:39–44; Luke 23:34–46; Luke 24:30–31; 1 Thessalonians 5:16–18; Matthew 14:17–21; John 17–18:9

3. FAITH
Facing the Unknown with Confidence

Introduction

1 Thessalonians 5:24; Matthew 17:20–21

Broken Dreams

Joshua 14:6–15; 2 Samuel 5:4–5; Genesis 37:2—50:26; Genesis 17:1–25—21:1–7; Matthew 7:7–11; Proverbs 13:12; Ecclesiastes 3:11

Step Out of the Boat

1 Corinthians 10:13; Matthew 14:22–23; Psalm 16:8

Uncharted Territory

2 Corinthians 5:7; Genesis 12:1–9; Jeremiah 29:11

A Purpose-Driven Woman

Luke 8:43–48; Matthew 6:33; Hebrews 11:6

Unlikely People

Hebrews 11:1–3; Philippians 4:13; Acts 9; Genesis 17:4; Genesis 21:5; Exodus 2:11–12; Exodus 4:10; Joshua 2;

4. OFFENSE
It's a Choice

The Mouth of the Lion

*Daniel 6:22; Proverbs 18:21; Numbers 12:1–16; James
3:7–16; Proverbs 11:27; Proverbs 31:26; James 3:7–18;
Proverbs 16:28; Ephesians 4:29*

The Prodigal

*Luke 15:11–32; Matthew 7:5; 1 John 1:8–9; John 6:7;
Ephesians 4:31–32; Ephesians 6:12; Romans 12:4–5;
Matthew 18:15–20; Proverbs 21:31; John 4:20; Galatians
5:13–15; 1 Corinthians 12:18–31; Ephesians 4:31–32;
2 Corinthians 3:18; Matthew 16:24; John 12:24–26; Luke
9:24–25; Proverbs 4:23; Acts 7:59–60*

He Would Have Passed By

Mark 6:48–51; Hebrews 3:7–8

Steps toward Forgiveness

*Matthew 7:12; Colossians 3:2; Matthew 5:44; Proverbs 4:23;
Proverbs 4:7; Psalm 34:1; James 1:5; Ephesians 5:1–2;
Romans 6:14; Hebrews 12:1; Romans 12:2; Romans 12:9–21*

5. MINDSET
What You Believe Will Either Hold You Captive
or Set You Free

Introduction

Luke 17:20–21; Matthew 4:17; Proverbs 23:7

Breaking Free

1 Corinthians 10:13; Acts 16:16–40; Matthew 16:19

Change of Heart

*Isaiah 43:18–19; Matthew 4:18–20; John 21:1–6;
Ephesians 4:22–24*

Loosed and Unbound

John 11:1–44; 2 Peter 2:19; Romans 8:37–39

Who's to Blame

*Luke 6:45; John 5:1–15; Philippians 2:14; Philippians 4:8;
Romans 12:2; Romans 14:12; Psalm 34:1–2; 2 Chronicles
24:20; Galatians 6:5; Matthew 25:14–30*

6. PROVISION
It's Always Been There

Dry Ground

Joshua 21:45; Proverbs 13:12; Exodus 17:1–7; Numbers 20:2–13; Exodus 14:11; Exodus 14:15–16; Joshua 3:5–17; Ecclesiastes 3:11; Matthew 13:15

The Wilderness Journey

Exodus 23:20; Exodus 35; Exodus 28:2; Exodus 16:11–16; Exodus 17; Isaiah 45:2–3

The Road of Despair

John 15:13; Luke 10:29–37; 2 Corinthians 4:7; Matthew 25:40

Can You Hear the Whisper?

Isaiah 41:10; 1 Kings 18–19; Philippians 4:6

False Evidence Appearing Real

Genesis 21:9–21; Deuteronomy 31:8; Psalm 37:25

A Jar of Oil

Psalm 37:25; James 4:2–3; 1 Samuel 30:6; 2 Kings 4:1–7; Proverbs 12:15; Matthew 6:25–27

Illegal Entry

John 16:33; 1 John 5:19; Philippians 1:27; Luke 12:7; Isaiah 53:5–6; 1 John 3:1–3;

7. IDENTITY
Discovering God's Plan for Your Life

Insufficient

Luke 18:27; John 6:1–13; 1 Samuel 16:7

What's in Your Hand?

Matthew 25:15–30; Galatians 6:4; Matthew 25:14–30; Galatians 6:4; Ecclesiastes 3:1–8; Exodus 2:1–10; Exodus 4:17; Exodus 1:2—2:23; Acts 7:20–22; 1 Samuel 17:34–37; 1 Samuel 16:23; 1 Samuel 17:50–53; 2 Samuel 6:1; 2 Samuel 5:4; 1 Kings 19:19–21; 2 Kings 2:9–15; Genesis 37:1–4; Genesis 37:23–28; Genesis 39:20–23; Genesis 41:41–46

One Stitch at a Time

Jeremiah 1:5; Psalm 139:13–16; Jeremiah 31:3;
1 Corinthians 10:13; Isaiah 43:2

The Original Design

Genesis 1:1; Genesis 1:27; Genesis 1:26–27; Jeremiah 29:11;
Romans 12:6; 2 Timothy 3:17; 1 Peter 5:6; John 10:29;
Isaiah 41:10; Psalm 32:8; 1 Corinthians15:33; Hebrews
10:24–25; 1 Thessalonians 5:11; John 3:16; Romans 12:2

Someone Else's Shoes

1 Corinthians 12:11–22; Romans 12:4–8

Kingdom Identity

Philippians 3:20; Philippians 1:27; Proverbs 23:7; Matthew
16:19; Matthew 6:33; Hosea 4:6; Matthew 22:1–14

Our Inheritance

Psalm 139:16; Matthew 7:11; 1 Corinthians 15:45–49;
Genesis 2:7; Romans 12:2; Isaiah 40:13; John 4:4–26;
Genesis 1:27–2:7; John 10:10; Romans 12:2; Matthew
5:13–14; Jeremiah 1:5; Hebrews 10:16–25; Ephesians 1:5;
John 1:11–13

A New Name

Hosea 12:3–5; Genesis 26:21–26; Genesis 31:3; Genesis
31—33:16

Steps to Discovering Your God-Given Identity

Psalm 119:105; 2 Timothy 3:16; Mark 12:30–31; John 4:23;
James 4:8; Jeremiah 29:13; Romans 12:2; Luke 17:5–6;
2 Timothy 1:7; John 16:13; Psalm 119:133; Philippians
4:6–7; 1 Corinthians 5:7; Proverbs 13:20; Hebrews 10:25;
Proverbs 1:5; Psalm 1:1; Hebrews 11:1; Matthew 6:33

ABOUT THE AUTHOR

Kathleen is the founder and director of Treasures of the Heart and Higher Ground Ministries. She holds credentials in biblical study and counsel and is licensed, ordained, and commissioned through Kingdom Mandate Fellowship (Global) in Omaha, Nebraska.

Her heart is to captivate others with the Word of God, encouraging them to cultivate intimacy with the person of the Holy Spirit and to teach them how to live from the place of rest with Him as they come into the knowledge of their true identity in Christ.

Kathleen has founded several ministries and has been instrumental in creating and developing Bible studies and prayer groups for all ages. With years of experience serving within the local church and surrounding area in almost every capacity, including Director of Women's Ministries, she has brought hope and encouragement to countless individuals.

Her sensitivity to the Holy Spirit enables her to prophesy accurately and discern spiritual strongholds, often leading to breakthrough for individuals, families, and ministries. Along with her prayer team, Kathleen spends countless hours cultivating God's presence through meditation and prayer, resulting in fresh revelation, empowerment, and anointing to the ministry. Her personal journey stands as a testament to God's healing power, and faithfulness. Her writings and teachings are inspired by a lifetime of experience and intimate time spent with the one true God.

Kathleen lives in Nebraska and is a wife, mother and grandmother to twelve beautiful grandchildren. She welcomes speaking engagements and invitations to share her testimony, insights, and passion for the transforming work of the Holy Spirit.

To contact Kathleen visit her website
www.treasuresoftheheartministries.com
K.Vonseggern@outlook.com

www.ingramcontent.com/pod-product-compliance
Lightning Source LLC
La Vergne TN
LVHW052017080426
835513LV00018B/2064